*A Soul-Chilling Journey
Behind the Psychic Curtain*

From California's infamous House of Curses to
the bizarre secret of Jayne Mansfield's tragic
death . . . The sadistic demon in Nashville who
tortures her victims with hellfire . . . Baltimore's
vengeful poltergeists wreaking havoc from
beyond the grave . . . Ghostly sex fiends that
defile innocent women . . . The eerie spectre
seen pacing the decks of Errol Flynn's pleasure
yacht . . . And the living nightmare that still
stalks the ruins of Jonestown—where 900
people took their own lives . . .

More Haunted Houses
An Incredible,
Fully-Documented Investigation
of the Most Baffling Mysteries
in the Psychic World

MORE
HAUNTED
HOUSES

BY RICHARD WINER
AND NANCY OSBORN ISHMAEL

MORE HAUNTED HOUSES
A Bantam Book | July 1981

ACKNOWLEDGMENTS

Lines from "When I am Dead" from *Lyric and Dramatic Poems* by John G. Neihardt; copyright 1915, 1916, 1919, 1921, 1926, by Macmillan Company, copyright © 1954 by John G. Neihardt. Published by Bison Books, University of Nebraska Press. By permission of the John G. Neihardt Trust.

Lines from "Sanctuary" from *The Collected Poems of Elinor Wylie* by Elinor Wylie; copyright 1921 by Alfred A. Knopf, Inc., copyright renewed 1949 by William Rose Benet. By permission of Alfred A. Knopf, Inc.

Excerpt from *Family Digest*, May 1974 issue; by permission of *Our Sunday Visitor*.

(Note: Every effort has been made to locate the copyright owners of material reproduced in this book. Ommissions brought to our attention will be corrected in subsequent editions.)

ISBN 0-553-14243-7

Published simultaneously in the United States and Canada

Bantam Books are published by Bantam Books, Inc. Its trademark, consisting of the words "Bantam Books" and the portrayal of a bantam, is Registered in U.S. Patent and Trademark Office and in other countries. Marca Registrada. Bantam Books, Inc., 666 Fifth Avenue, New York, New York 10103.

PRINTED IN THE UNITED STATES OF AMERICA

0 9 8 7 6 5 4 3 2 1

Acknowledgments

William Bailey Allen
Mildred Cowan
Naomi Graybeal, Department of Tourism, Frankfort, Ky.
Amelia Allen Hartz, author of compilation of Kentucky
  folklore
Debbie Herrick, Ft. Lauderdale, Fla.
Jack Midkiff, W. Frankfort, Ill.
Debbie Reeser, Deerfield, Fla.
Marge Serkin, Margate, Fla.
Robert H. Shepphard
WHAS-TV, Louisville, Ky.

Contents

MORE
HAUNTED
HOUSES

Tell me not in mournful numbers,
Life is but an empty dream!
For the soul is dead that slumbers,
And things are not what they seem."
                    Henry W. Longfellow
                    (*A Psalm of Life*)

1

The House of Curses

Late at night, as the fog rolls in across the San Francisco
Bay and the air turns cold, the people turn off their lights
and go to sleep. But in one of those darkened houses—a
house that looks much like the others, except for the fact
that it was once painted black—the occupants are not
asleep. Nor are they under the realm of Morpheus. For the
structure is reigned over by Satan.

What was once the living room now serves as a chamber for ceremonies of the Devil. As the Satanic Mass
commences, about twenty people sit in a semicircle before
a combination fireplace-altar constructed from ballast
stones of old sailing ships. A black coffin stands on end in
one corner of the room. In the opposite corner is a golden
mummy case bearing the carved likeness of a long-dead
Egyptian king. Candles are lit—thirteen black and one
white—and the lights are turned off. The black candles
are used to burn parchments on which requests for bless-
ings have been written; the lone white candle is used to
burn parchments upon which curses have been penned.
The flickering candlelight is readily absorbed by the
blood-red ceiling and black walls of the chamber.

The male participants wear black robes, some of which are hooded. The women also wear black, but their garments are sexually suggestive.

Suddenly the grim silence is broken by the ear-shattering sound of a bell rung by the cult's High Priestess, an attractive woman with long blond hair. The bell, rung to purify the air of all extraneous sounds, signals the beginning of the ritual. An organist plays the eerie strains of a dirge by Bach. As the participants rise, the Black Pope of the Church of Satan enters. He wears a cap with two protruding bone horns, and with his long pointed ears, triangular goatee, and black Fu Manchu mustache, his appearance is strikingly satanic. He cradles a bundle wrapped in a leopard skin in his arms. The exotic covering falls to one side momentarily to reveal the face of a beautiful blonde woman. Her fair skin and extraordinary beauty present an erotic but ghastly contrast to the High Priest's black robes and macabre appearance. She will serve as a living altar during the rituals and incantations.

The woman is carried across the dimly lit chamber and is gently placed on the stone altar, of which she becomes a part. The leopard skin is peeled back, exposing an utterly flawless nude body. The participants murmur "Hail, Satan," in awed tribute. Then a gong is sounded to call upon the forces of darkness.

The naked woman who has become a human altar is the subject of fantasy for millions of movie-goers around the world. But this is not a movie set. It is for real. Only her most intimate friends are aware of the dark, secret side of her life.

The Black Pope continues the rite, "In the name of Satan, the Ruler of the earth, the King of the world, I command the forces of Darkness to bestow their infernal power upon me!" The naked woman reposing upon the altar appears even more strikingly beautiful as the dim candlelight enhances even the slightest movement. The heretofore motionless body of Vera Jayne Palmer begins to throb visibly as the ritual reaches a fiery climax. *"Hail, Satan!"*

Vera Jayne Palmer, better known as Jayne Mansfield, was deeply involved in the blackest of the occult arts at the time of her death in 1966. Her pink, thirty-seven-room Bel-Air mansion, built in the 1920s by entertainer Rudy Vallee, but never lived in by him, was often the site of séances, coven meetings, and other mystical ceremonies. It is a part of her life that the producers of a recent television special neglected to disclose. In fact, all but one of her many biographers have shied away from the more bizarre aspects of Jayne Mansfield's life. Although her friends warned her that she was playing with fire, Jayne continued to experiment with the black arts.

Jayne Mansfield was one of America's top pinup girls, and her movie studio was grooming her to be another Marilyn Monroe. Crowds thronged around her wherever she went, and she was making an enormous amount of money. She lacked nothing—except happiness. Jayne and her estranged third husband, Matt Cimber, were in the middle of a child-custody suit, and the turmoil was rapidly consuming her. Divorce proceedings had been under way for some time. And, to further complicate matters, her attorney, Sam Brody, was not only ripping her off, but blackmailing her, according to Anton LaVey.

Jayne first met Anton Szandor LaVey during the 1966 San Francisco International Film Festival, after she had read some newspaper stories about him and his San Francisco–based Church of Satan. Jayne was enthralled with the philosophy, theatrical trappings, and basic concepts of Satanism. She began attending the satanic rituals on a regular basis, usually flying up from Los Angeles. Sometimes she accompanied LaVey on his investigations of haunted houses in the Bay Area.

One can imagine the scene as America's number-one sex symbol was met at the airport by a diabolical-looking man in sinister black garb. After fighting their way through the celebrity-hungry crowds, they would enter LaVey's black Jaguar sedan and, with the back seat full of Jayne's pink* luggage, drive to the black house on California Street. Once away from the airport, Jayne's privacy was of the utmost importance. Sometimes her arrival at the sanctuary was timed to occur after dark;

---

*Everything that Jayne Mansfield owned that could be made pink, was pink—luggage, cars, house, furnishings, etc.

other times, a hat and veil shielded her. Even the bedroom in which she stayed was entered through a secret opening in the wall. Much of the secrecy was maintained because of Sam Brody, Jayne's companion and attorney.

Jayne sought counseling from LaVey. She confided to him that on several occasions Brody had drugged her and taken nude pictures of her lying in bed with strange men. He had threatened to "release the pictures to the right people" in her child-custody suit. Thus, he was able to gain sexual favors from her. It was also discovered that Brody had been double-billing her for his services and stealing both money and jewelry from her.

LaVey told Jayne that Brody's treachery was a problem she would have to solve herself, but he would show her the way. Thus, Jayne Mansfield, who had already been a student of the occult arts, became one of the Church of Satan's more enthusiastic members in 1966; eventually, she became a priestess.

We were granted an interview with the Black Pope of the Church of Satan in June 1980. Sworn to secrecy regarding the exact location, we were afforded the rare opportunity of encountering LaVey in his home in the north of San Francisco.

For those who are not familiar with LaVey, he is a well-proportioned six-footer attired all in black except for a maroon-striped tie. That was our first look at Anton Szandor LaVey. He is a most devilish-looking man. The study's backlighting gave his long pointed ears a translucent, reddish neon quality. As LaVey's lips parted in a half-smile, I saw long, sharply pointed, glistening white teeth. If any practitioner of the black arts looks the role of the Evil One, it is certainly Anton LaVey. After the initial shock, however, he seemed quite pleasant. He greeted us in a soft-toned, masculine voice and formally introduced himself. When Diane, LaVey's wife, returned with our coffee, the interview began.

After he explained how Jayne Mansfield had become involved in the Church of Satan, I asked about the notorious curse that supposedly led to her death and that of her companion.

LaVey replied, "Contrary to what several uninformed

sources have said, there never was a curse placed on Jayne Mansfield. She was an active member in good standing with the Church of Satan until the very end. In fact, when she was killed, she was wearing her Baphomet.* It was one that we had made especially for her, pink-enameled.

"Actually, the curse you mention was placed on Sam Brody, Jayne's attorney. He'd been giving her a rough time and even embarrassing her in public. At the San Francisco International Film Festival, he threw liquor all over her dress. He was enraged at her enthusiasm for the Church of Satan. He had blackened her eyes and beaten her up on many occasions."

"What was the curse that you put on Brody?" I asked.

"The death curse—because he was a pest, a nuisance; he wouldn't leave her alone. Brody was probably so deeply emotionally involved with her that he couldn't control himself. He might have been a very kind, sweet man at one time. But passion can do strange things to people. . . . He threatened me and set up very unpleasant situations. In other words, he tried to make my life as unbearable as possible.

"Brody followed Jayne everywhere she went, despite her attempts to shake him. He'd find out when she was coming to see me, and then he'd take an earlier flight so that he would be there waiting when she disembarked. Jayne unloaded her problems with Brody on me daily. When she returned from San Francisco, furniture would be missing from her home, or she'd find bills for services that had not been authorized or in some cases not even performed. Brody padded his statements and sometimes double-billed her.

"Actually, Brody had her in a very delicate position. Supposedly, he represented her legally, but he had her so compromised that she couldn't leave him. He arranged that she was so deeply in debt to him for legal services that if he had demanded payment, the consequences would have been terrible. And if she didn't conform to his personal wishes, he threatened to have custody of her

---

*An emblem containing a five-point star with a satanic figure centered in the middle and surrounded by a circle, worn as a brooch or necklace.

children withdrawn—have her declared an unfit mother. As an attorney, he could probably have accomplished that, too."

"How do you put a curse on someone?" I asked.

"I had previously placed two death curses on persons, but it was very spontaneous in this case, because he threatened me over the telephone. He had just finished beating Jayne up, breaking the door down, and making a big scene. She was screaming for help over the telephone —crying pitifully. He took the phone from her and told me that I was never to speak to Jayne again. He said if I continued to befriend her or even to answer her calls, he would expose me as a charlatan and instigate all sorts of legal actions against me.

"I got very angry and told him that he had underestimated me because up to that point I had been a gentleman, for Jayne's sake. I had taken a lot of verbal abuse from him, and I'd seen others take his verbal and physical abuse, but I hadn't done anything about it. Finally, I felt Brody should be warned that he was dealing with greater powers than he'd ever dreamed of and that all his threats would amount to nothing. I said to him, 'Go ahead, expose and attack me and be damned, because in a year you'll be dead.' It was as simple as that. He just slammed the phone down without saying another word.

"A few minutes later, Jayne called back. Apparently Sam was worried, because he got on the phone and said, 'All is forgiven. Just forget what I said. Everything is all right.' But I replied that things were not all right. 'You did things in the church you shouldn't have done. You disrupted the services, rearranged and lit our ceremonial candles, and committed atrocious impieties. I even had to call the police to forcibly eject you on several occasions. No,' I said, 'it's not all right.' "

When asked if anyone had tried to warn Jayne not to take Brody with her on that fatal trip, LaVey replied, "I did. I told her. She knew the effectiveness of the curse, too. She just couldn't shake him.

"I warned her to stay away from him [Brody]. I pleaded with Jayne, begged her to avoid the man. I explained that Brody was traveling under a dark cloud and there was no way he could escape. But she wouldn't listen. She just wouldn't listen."

LaVey was referring to two automobile accidents that Brody had while Jayne was with him. One occurred on a Monday morning in mid-June at the intersection of Sunset and Whittier in Beverly Hills. Although Jayne escaped injury, Brody suffered a broken leg, a broken elbow and thumb, and two cracked teeth. His late-model Mercedes was demolished.

Both his leg and arm were in casts when, a week later, Jayne and Brody were involved in another car accident. They were in San Francisco, and Brody had refused to allow Jayne to ride in LaVey's black Jaguar. Neither suffered injuries from that mishap. Still, Jayne would not heed Anton LaVey's warning to stay away from the accursed Sam Brody.

A week later, in the early-morning hours of June 29, 1967, after finishing her evening performance at Gus Steven's Supper Club in Biloxi, Mississippi, Jayne, three of her children, Sam Brody, and the club's driver, nineteen-year-old Ron Harrison, started driving to New Orleans, where she was scheduled to appear on a television talk show later that morning. Jayne stood nearby as the kids and the luggage were packed into the car. She looked tired, haggard, and hungover. Harrison was driving, with Brody in the middle of the front seat, and Jayne sat beside him, next to the door.

As the children slept in the back seat, the 1966 Buick sedan raced west along Route 90. The road was slick from a light rain that had started falling earlier. Ahead, Harrison saw a large white cloud coming from a mosquito-spraying truck. He slowed down and followed the truck for several minutes, then became impatient, accelerated, and drove around the spray truck into the fog. It was 2:25 A.M.

Since childhood, Jayne had had a fear of driving in the rain. It probably began when she was riding with her parents through a rainstorm in eastern Pennsylvania. Her father suddenly slumped over the wheel and died instantly. Fortunately, Jayne's mother was able to grab the wheel and guide the car to a safe stop. It is very probable that Jayne was haunted by that tragic experience while driving in the rain with Harrison and Brody that night.

On June 28, in an orchid-colored house in Dallas, Texas, Jayne's mother, Vera Peers, suddenly sat up in bed. A nightmare had startled her out of a sound sleep. In it, Jayne had called to her, "Mama, Mama, come here. I want you, Mother."

When Vera Peers went back to sleep, her daughter again appeared and took her by the hand. "She was smiling," said Mrs. Peers. "She was wearing a black hat, and so was I. She told me, 'You must be careful, Mama. I will help you. We are going down those steps.' We were standing at the top of some marble stairs, beautiful ones with birds and angels carved in them. There were hundreds of beautiful steps. There were many people gathered at the bottom, and Jayne said, 'Don't worry, Mother, I know those people and I'm going to introduce you to them.'"

About that point in her dream, Vera was awakened by a knock on the door. She and her husband answered it. "Mrs. Peers," a Texas State Trooper said, "I have some very bad news for you. Your daughter, Jayne Mansfield, has been involved in a serious automobile accident."

Harrison did not know that a slow-moving trailer truck was ahead of him until the hood of the Buick slammed under it. The top of the Buick was sheared off as though it were a giant sardine can. Sam Brody died instantly when he was thrown from the car. Harrison suffered the same fate. The children in the back seat were alive but sustained injuries.

When the truck driver, who was unhurt, leaped from his cab, he saw the bodies of two men sprawled on the pavement. Glancing at the Buick's windshield, he saw the bloodied head of a blond woman gaping through the smashed glass. Then, looking back to the roadway, he saw a woman's body. His eyes scanned from the blue boots to the blue mini-dress, past the blood-soaked blouse, to the shoulders. His gaze stopped abruptly. There was no head.

LaVey later declared that "Jayne was the victim of her own frivolity." Many members of California's occult underground were of the opinion that LaVey's curse got out of control, killing both the disciple and the nonbeliever.

Shortly after Jayne's death, a memorial service was held at the Church of Satan. About thirty persons were present. Halfway through the ritual, the amber-colored bulbs suddenly flared up. The lights didn't merely become brighter but rather blazed to the intensity of photoflood bulbs for almost half a minute. It was as though there had been an immense increase in the voltage. Yet, the filaments, which should have burned out from such a sudden surge in voltage, were undamaged, and the bulbs were still usable. One of the glaring bulbs—the one over the altar—flared up into a heart-shaped form, which was Jayne's favorite design. The swimming pools, bathtubs, and other possessions at her home were heart-shaped. Asked whether he had anything to do with the spontaneous flaring of the lights, LaVey replied, "Anyone can rig bulbs to flare up like that, but to do so without damaging them is impossible. I think Jayne wanted to let us know that she is still with us."

After Jayne's tragic departure from this world, her estate became the subject of considerable legal dispute between legitimate heirs, would-be heirs, and freeloaders. Everyone wanted a piece of the action—her children, estranged husband, ex-husband, business associates, Brody's wife, attorneys. Lawyers later declared that no less than six hundred thousand dollars of the million-dollar estate would be spent in legal fees and expenses. Martha Saxton, in her biography of Jayne Mansfield, referred to the fiasco as a "lawyers' picnic." As the rightful heirs watched their shares dwindle, other unexplainable things were happening.

Linda Mudrick, Jayne's personal maid, had on a number of occasions heard Miklos, Jayne's oldest son, who saw his mother's decapitated body at the accident scene, talking to someone when she knew he was alone in his room. He told her, "I've been talking with Mommy. She comes here a lot to visit me." The maid's reaction was that Jayne was calling on her son from the spirit world.

Other bizarre occurrences were happening in or around the Pink Palace. Mickey Hargitay, Jayne's second husband, had a bad car accident just after driving out the gate. Third husband Matt Cimber, who was estranged from her at the time of her death, began having his share of troubles too. His father had a heart attack, legal problems were falling upon his newly acquired nightclub, and his best friend was killed. Then Linda herself was involved in a serious auto crash.

One day a plaque appeared on the wall of Jayne's pink bedroom over her heart-shaped bed. It was a certificate from Anton LaVey's Church of Satan, proclaiming Jayne a priestess. No one knows how it got there. LaVey hadn't been in the house during that time.

Victor Huston, a relatively young man who was Jayne's road manager and a constant visitor at the Pink Palace, died suddenly.

Two of Jayne's children, Miklos and Maria, both of whom survived the fatal car wreck, were playing in a toy electric car one afternoon in the mansion's playground. Maria leaned back and somehow her long black hair became entangled around an axle. All of the hair on the back of her head was torn out by the roots.

Bursting water pipes spoiled much of the furnishings. Plumbers who repaired the damage became frightened by mysteriously moving objects. One painter said that whenever he was working in Jayne's room, he felt that he was not alone, even though no one else was in the room. Several times he actually felt someone touch him on the shoulder. Eerie moaning sounds emanated seemingly from nowhere.

Servants refused to stay on. New ones were hired but left after spending only a few days in the house. Even Linda Mudrick, the maid, left, saying, "I never want to go into that house again."

Could Jayne, in another dimension, have been aware of what was being done to her estate and her children's inheritance? It is possible.

May Mann, a columnist who was working on a biography of Jayne* and had all but the last few chapters finished at the time of the actress's death, told of numerous visits by Jayne's ghost while the last two chapters

---

*Jayne Mansfield—A Biography. Drake, New York, N.Y.

were being written. She heard Jayne's voice: "Please! Please! Please! You promised!" Mann was repeatedly urged to complete the biography; the ghostly voice insisted that she wanted the world to know "the truth about me and my life."

On another occasion, Ms. Mann locked the manuscript up for the night. No one else had access to it. Yet, when she took it out the following day to resume writing, she was horrified to find blood splattered between nearly all of the pages. This occurred at the same time that she was writing about Jayne's fatal accident.

In the August 1978 issue of *Death,* a monthly tabloid that thrived on sensationalism, reporter Steve Becker interviewed Grey Tyler, an author, playwright, and intimate of many Hollywood celebrities. According to the article, after sacking the pink Bel-Air mansion, Jayne's estranged husband Matt Cimber and his lawyers locked out the children and Jayne's parents, then sold the place. There have been five different tenants in the thirty-seven room structure since Jayne's death. The first occupants were a bank president and his family. Right after they moved in, the banker's eighteen-year-old son found a pink Honda that the late actor Nick Adams had bought Jayne after a brief affair. The boy started it up and took it for a spin around the estate, then decided to try it on the road. Roaring out past the iron gates and onto Sunset Boulevard, he was struck by a car and killed. The banker and his family moved out the same day.

Singing star "Mama" Cass Elliot, a celebrity of the 1960s, was not associated with the occult. Not long after moving into the stately mansion, she went to London to tape some commercials, leaving her husband behind to oversee the redecorating of the mansion. Although she was thousands of miles from the house, she wasn't far enough away to escape the wrath that apparently was emanating from it. During her stay in London, she choked to death on a ham sandwich. Needless to say, her husband vacated the premises.

Another tenant—after moving in—began to experience some strange phenomena, as stated in the *Death* write-up. When alone, she had a feeling that she wasn't alone. She constantly felt an urge to bleach her hair, which she finally did after three weeks of restraint. One rainy afternoon, as she was poking through the basement, she discovered a trunk full of Jayne's clothes. After rummaging through the chest for several hours, she returned upstairs.

That night she was awakened by an urge to return to the cellar. Sleepy-eyed, she donned her robe and walked down the steps. With no forethought whatsoever, she went directly to the trunk. Soon she found herself trying on practically every garment in the trunk.

The garments didn't fit her too well. Thus, later that day she took some of the garments to a seamstress for alterations. Next, she went to a plastic surgeon to arrange for a breast enlargement. When questioned by her friends, she responded that it was just something she had to do; she could give no reason for the compulsion.

Soon, anything to do with Jayne Mansfield became an obsession with her. Whenever she heard of some Jayne Mansfield memorabilia being offered for sale, she would rush off and buy it. Then she had her bleached hair restyled to look like Jayne's. It was as though she was possessed by the late actress.

But that was not to be—for long. One night she woke and heard a woman's querulous voice calling to her, "Get out. Get out!" Aware of the fate that befell the previous two tenants, she packed up her belongings and fled from the pink mansion.

The next occupant of the Pink Palace, according to Becker's article, was none other than Ringo Starr of Beatle fame. (The Beatles, incidentally, were ardent fans of Jayne Mansfield while she was alive and were acquainted with her on a first-name basis.) Although Ringo used the house mainly for parties and actually lived in it only for a short while, he had the entire exterior of the pink house repainted white. But the house began turning pink again. Some claimed that the reason was that pink is a hard color to cover with white paint. Others blamed it on the quality of the white paint. And then, there were those who attributed it to Jayne's energetic presence.

Again the house was repainted, using a sealer and two coats of white paint. But once again the house returned to pink. Paint consultants and chemists were unable to explain the phenomenon. Eventually, the house was successfully repainted, for it is no longer pink.

Next to occupy the mansion was a member of the Church of Satan who held regular satanic rituals within its walls. The Satanists never experienced any terrifying moments in the house. But Satanists deal with bizarre mysteries most of the time, and eerie happenings don't shake them. However, they admitted to feeling the constant presence of Jayne during their stay in the manor. It is possible that practitioners of the black arts are fully capable of restraining spirits from the other world, especially when the entity is one of their own. Too, it is possible that the disciples of the forces of darkness were responsible for Jayne's hauntings and kept her around as long as they needed her. Or perhaps they were attempting to recompense for the black curse on Sam Brody that erroneously claimed the actress, too. It is also possible that Jayne just wanted her presence known by the Satanists because of her friendship with them during the last year of her life. Whatever the reason, the hauntings had diminished by the time the next occupant took over.

Engelbert Humperdinck, who, ironically, was once involved romantically with Jayne, purchased the mansion in 1977. Before he moved in, Humperdinck had a Catholic priest bless the house. In a statement issued by his press agent in June 1980, Humperdinck said, "I am very aware of the fact that other people have speculated about my home, but I have never found anything that would validate them." He was replying to a question as to whether the house was still haunted. However, he added that after a recent earthquake, the ground settled, exposing a heart-shaped configuration—Jayne's favorite pattern. Upon investigation, it was discovered to be a filled-in wading pool that Jayne had built for her children.

Haunted houses and ghosts—the hills of Hollywood are full of them. Most of those who share their homes with spiritual inhabitants and are aware of the situation have a tendency to deny such activities, probably out of fear of how others will interpret their admission of ghostly experiences. But there is ample evidence that Hollywood is a haven for haunters.

When your soft cheeks by perfumed winds are fanned,
'Twill be my kiss—and you will understand.
But when some sultry, storm-bleared sun has set,
I will be lightning if you dare forget!

John G. Neihardt
(*When I Am Dead*)

2

The Lady

I came to the gloomy frame house on Sharp Street in East Nashville, Tennessee, expecting to interview the Haywood family and in particular Ann Haywood, a woman possessed by the awesome presence of "the Lady."

However, the middle-aged woman who opened the door informed me that the Haywood family had moved out. She went on to explain that the ferocious psychic attacks seemed to be centered in the house on Sharp Street. The Haywoods had moved away in hopes of lessening the severity of the psychic assaults of "the Lady," and the house had been converted to a nursing home for the mentally ill and the senile.

My research into one of the most shocking and controversial cases of phenomenal happenings had begun. In a large frame home in East Nashville, Ann Haywood, her husband, Dorris, and their six children had come under brutal psychic attack by a force so hideous in appearance and so evil in action that it can be justifiably described as demonic. And, in spite of the Haywood family's move from the house, the haunter still pursues them.

The assaults of "the Lady" on Ann Haywood's person

15

have been numerous and terrifying. The fiendish spirit has burned Ann's tongue so severely that she could not speak for several days. It has hovered over her, placing its mouth upon hers, and pulled the very breath from her body. "The Lady" delights in scorching Ann's skin and often strikes her face, leaving it swollen and bruised. The entity tortures her with unpleasant insights into the future. Once, it took Ann's spirit completely from her body, leaving what was apparently a corpse. Only emergency efforts saved her life. Ann continues to experience great trauma and has become very ill due to the visitations of the malevolent spirit.

It was a hot summer night in 1975 when "the Lady" first manifested. A cool breeze came through the window of the bedroom where Ann lay restlessly beside her husband, who was sleeping. The breeze felt good, but Ann was experiencing some discomfort resulting from recent surgery and could not fall asleep. When the sheer curtains billowed out in an unusually strong gust of wind, Ann thought that perhaps a summer thunderstorm was about to strike. A sudden chill enveloped the room. She turned to look out the window for some sign of rain. The thing she saw at that moment would change her whole life.

"There was this form—that's all I can call it—and it came in through the window," Ann recounted, her eyes widening in relived terror at the memory of that first encounter. "That was the beginning of a hell for me.

"It was a woman—I still think of her only as 'the Lady'—and she was accompanied by two children. There was a dresser between the two windows and the children stayed there. I really couldn't tell what she looked like until she came to the foot of the bed. I was praying that I'd wake up, even though I knew I wasn't asleep. She kept coming, and then I got a good look at her for the first time. How well I know her now!

"How can I stand this! I thought. I tried to wake my husband, but he was sound asleep.

"I could see that she had on a cape. Out from under the cape—I know this sounds preposterous—came two hands. No body, just two hands. They were just like pig's feet.

"She had no distinct age. Her face was almond-shaped,

her ears were pointed and came around, and her mouth was more like a rat's than anything else I can think of. Her hair was all on top, almost like a flat-top. And her eyes! Intense, like fire. Her children looked the same.

"She told me that she had come for me, that I was due to go with her. I began to pray out loud—'Lord, this has to be a dream. Let me wake up!'

"This didn't disturb her. She moved closer. 'You won't have to suffer anymore. You won't have to worry anymore. . . .' "

(It had been a bad year for Ann and her family. In 1975 the construction industry was in a slump and Ann's husband, a subcontractor, found few jobs while their expenses soared. Ann's declining health was also a matter of great concern, as was the welfare of their six children.)

"The Lady moved closer. Then she stopped, and I stopped praying. 'You and your damned God. You don't need God. You're with me.'

"All I could think was, This can't be happening! The medication they've given me has knocked me out. But all I had been given was penicillin.

"She moved even closer to me and spread her cape across me. When she did that, I felt a peace like I'd never felt before in my life. She's done it many times since, and every time she does, I feel an incredible calmness.

"When she came close to my face, I was frightened, but at the same time I felt that I was *with* her—that I was totally hers. She came down over my mouth and began to take my breath. You know how you get short of breath when you run?—it was like that. Then I began to fight her—I felt like she was trying to kill me. When she backed off, I began to pray again. 'There's no God,' she said. 'I'm your peace, I'm your strength, and I'll take care of you.'

"Then, without another word, she left."

Ann no longer sees the two children that accompanied the Lady on the first visitation. "I don't know what has happened to the children," said Ann. "I've tried to ask, but the Lady seems impatient at the question. I get the impression that they're off pursuing their own victims."

The Lady sometimes reacts like an incubus—a sexual

ghost. She often becomes very jealous of Ann's husband and anyone else who deprives her of Ann's attention, including Ann's six children. The Lady's fits of jealousy have led Ann to the brink of suicide.

"She has a temper, and when she's mad, she sometimes touches me violently. It feels like dry ice—you know, burning but at the same time cold. And she always wants to take my breath. She seems to need it."

In retrospect, Ann feels that the haunting began several weeks before the first manifestation. Ann entered the hospital as a surgery patient. She shared a room with an elderly woman who was dying. The woman was aware that Ann was there, but she remained silent for several days.

"Then the woman turned to me and began to move her lips. But no sound came out. I was puzzled. I told her I'd try to call the nurses, and I did. And then the woman said, very distinctly, 'You're doomed to hell.' Just as she said that, her eyes locked on me and she died.

"When the nurses came—it seemed like a long time, but it always does—they moved me into the hall while they took care of the body. They told me later that I had gone into shock. All I know is that when the woman spoke, I felt like a big weight was placed on me."

Ann and her family know that the Lady is always near. "They've never seen her, but they can feel her presence when she's with me," Ann said.

Actually, son Donnie came the closest to seeing the Lady. In spring of 1978, he saw something so frightful in the hall that he fled in terror. "Mom wasn't there," he said. "The eyes were shining in the hall, like balls of fire."

Ronnie, Ann's eighteen-year-old son, said, "I've never seen her, but I can feel her presence by the chill. I haven't talked to many people about it—they'd just think I'm crazy." When asked if he's afraid of the entity, he replied, "No, because she'd never hurt me." However, Ronnie did admit that he'd prefer it to go away and leave the family in peace.

The younger Haywood children accept the existence of the entity and appear to be happy and well adjusted.

Dorris, Ann's husband, admits that while he has never

seen the creature, he has no doubt that it exists. "I've seen what she's done to Ann. I've seen the marks on her face, which could not have been self-inflicted, and I've seen the overturned furniture. I've seen her frightened almost to the point of hysteria. I'm convinced she is possessed by this spirit."

In addition to physical assaults that have marked Ann Haywood's flesh, sounds are heard and objects are moved and broken in plain view of witnesses.

Others besides family members have sensed the presence of the Lady. There is a strange, pervasive coolness in the air when the Lady is around. "Once, in a hospital, a woman told me she saw something hovering over me— and I hadn't mentioned my problem to her," said Ann.

Ann has been examined many times by highly qualified doctors, including an eminent Nashville psychiatrist. (The Lady became very angry when Ann sought professional help.) However, psychiatric treatment was discontinued because Ann proved to function normally in her daily life.

Ann has resigned herself to the presence of the Lady. "I accept the fact that the Lady will be with me until I die," she said.

The Lady wants to claim Ann Haywood for her own, and, barring murder, she desires to manipulate every facet of Ann's life. But Ann resists this.

"Sometimes it gets to be ridiculous. A few days ago I was out shopping with a friend. I was looking at a bedspread when the Lady became so impatient to leave that she snatched the spread out of my hands. The woman I was with was startled. Fortunately, I've known her for a long time, and she remembers how terrified I was when I was first bothered by the Lady."

One of the most horrifying aspects of the haunting is the Lady's compulsion to descend upon Ann and suck her breath. "I don't know why I don't resist that," said Ann, "but I don't seem able to."

Stealing Ann's willpower played an important part in the near-death of the entire Haywood family during the early days of the haunting.

"She had appeared earlier in the day, and I was very upset. But then I heard a voice—a man's voice this time—that told me to turn off the gas jets in the living-room fireplace and then to turn them back on, 'then go back to bed and lie down and all your problems will be gone.' I did just that. I had no idea at the time that I was about to end my life and the lives of my family. But my husband woke up and asked me what was the matter. I tried to reassure him and tell him to go back to sleep, but he smelled the gas.

"It was then that I first told him about the Lady. There were several days of bad experiences after that."

The entity repeatedly brought a tiny white coffin decorated with nine pale yellow roses and presented it to Ann. "I was especially upset because my daughter was pregnant at the time and I feared that this somehow represented the child. I was puzzled, too, because the roses had no fragrance.

"And then it happened. My niece—only three weeks old at the time—died a crib death. It was completely unexpected. There was a white casket (it was the only one available), and a relative brought nine roses—not a dozen or a half-dozen—to place on the casket. When someone told me they were plastic—and without fragrance—that was too much."

Dorris Haywood confirmed the incident. The visitation, including the casket and roses, was related to him well before the infant's death.

The effect of the fulfilled prophecy was devastating to Ann. "I was so upset, I asked to be taken home from the funeral," she said. "I lay down, and the Lady came to me. She said, 'You see what power I have over you.' I had to agree.

"Then she put the cape over me and I left with her. I died physically—I know I did, because I could look back on my body lying in bed, while my husband and two of our children worked on me, trying to revive me."

Dorris Haywood verified her deathlike condition. "I couldn't feel any pulse, and there was no breathing. I began heart massage and mouth-to-mouth resuscitation. Two of the children, terrified, came to help."

During the resuscitation, Ann was in an out-of-body state. She hovered nearby, watching the whole procedure. "The cape was around me and I felt warm and secure. I knew I couldn't leave them, although I felt very good where I was."

Her husband said, "It was like a miracle. One minute she seemed dead, and then she was back again."

Because physicians and psychiatrists have failed to relieve Ann's affliction, other measures have been undertaken. Ministers from many religious organizations have prayed with her; exorcisms have been attempted. A minister from Greenville, Tennessee, attempted to lay the spirit, but as he prayed over Ann, his ceramic cross broke, apparently by itself.

"I've dealt with dozens of similar cases, and I'm fully convinced she was possessed," said the minister. "I think it was the struggle between good and evil that caused the cross to break."

Another minister contacted by the Haywood family commented, "She is possessed of Satan himself."

Recently, a renowned authority on demonology was brought to her by a relative. "He was delayed for some reason, and by the time he arrived, it was midnight. A thunderstorm came up, and there was lightning and hard rain—a good setting for what he was doing, I thought. He prayed and I prayed. He told me he could feel the presence of the Lady although he couldn't see her. When we were through, he told me she was gone forever.

"Unfortunately, she wasn't. She was just angry—very, very angry."

Recently, two writers who were investigating the mysterious happenings came in direct contact with the incredible being known as "the Lady"—and were nearly killed.

"It was a frightening experience . . . and because of it, I decided not to have anything more to do with the whole situation," said one of them.

Her associate, a seasoned reporter for WSM-TV in Nashville, said, "The Lady tried to kill us. She appeared to us outside the car—through the windshield—and tried to take possession of the car."

Two news reporters for the *Nashville Tennessean* who were writing a feature about the Lady had an incredible experience. An editor for that newspaper said, "I'm convinced we're dealing with something beyond our normal knowledge."

An associate editor for the same newspaper agreed. "There's no question that Mrs. Haywood is telling the truth. We got a psychiatrist to examine her, and he says she is absolutely normal."

Although the Lady has assured Ann Haywood that she is not bothered by publication of her story—in fact, she seems rather anxious for the attention—there are those at the *Tennessean* who have their doubts.

"The original interview with Mrs. Haywood was recorded on professional equipment, part of an integrated dictation system made by Lanier, on a professional Sony tape. The machine tore the tape up—the first time ever for this equipment to fail.

"After the story was reconstructed from notes, it was entered into the *Tennessean*'s editorial computer. The computer failed immediately, and had to be reset—twice! When the editing of the story was begun on a video-display terminal, that unit failed also, and the entire power-supply section had to be replaced. Another terminal was used."

Ann Haywood, who now faces an uncertain future with the added burden of a debilitating physical ailment, stated, "I've come to accept that she will be with me all my life. My family has also accepted that, although they don't like it.

"I've never made a secret of the Lady," said Ann, "but, since most people don't believe it anyway, I haven't exactly broadcast it."

The entity itself has told Ann, "Nobody will believe it." And the creature appears to be correct. Yet, Ann Haywood has told her story for a purpose. "There must be many other people who've had a similar experience. It may help them to learn that it is possible to live with such a thing."

Ann speaks to the Lady often, and the entity replies distinctly and coherently. However, such verbal communication is unnecessary, as the Lady can read Ann's every thought.

For the past six months or so, I have watched with fascination the metamorphosis of the Lady. In a recent phone conversation, Ann Haywood spoke in terms not unlike affection when telling of the visitations. "The Lady is only bad when I won't listen to her. It's like a mother-child relationship. A mother must correct a child to keep it from getting hurt, and what the Lady does is try to get my attention by making me follow her advice. When she tells me something, she's usually right."

"What, then, was the horrible business that happened at the Sharp Street address?" I asked.

"I'm glad you asked that, because now I finally understand it. There's something evil in the house. The Lady was the only barrier between that negative force and myself.

"She helps us now that we've moved away from Sharp Street. The Lady works with me on my music. She knows I like to compose music. There are many little ways she guides my family and I."

"Do you still think she's a demon?" I asked.

There was a pause before Ann replied, "She's from another dimension, but I don't think she's a demon. I'm not even sure what a demon is or if there really are such things. I do know that the Lady has a good side."

Though thou seest me not pass by, Thou shalt feel me
with thine eye as a thing that, though unseen,
Must be near thee, and hath been; And when in that
secret dread, Thou has turned around thy head, Thou
shalt marvel I am not as thy shadow on the spot,
And the power which thou dost feel . . . Shall be what
thou must conceal.

Lord Byron
"Sanctuary"

3

Ghosts with a Sex Drive

"Carlotta was sinking into helpless death, but she felt
huge hands on her knees, her legs, and then some knowledge floated like a shot up through her consciousness and
she understood and it filled her with energy. It filled her
with a savage strength. She bucked and kicked. Her arms
flailed, and when she bucked again to kick, to kill if she
had to, a searing pain ripped through her lower back,
rendering her powerless. Her legs were pinned onto the
bed. Carlotta felt ripped apart. She jerked her face, her
nose felt air, her mouth gasped and sucked in oxygen at
the side of the pillow. There was a scream. It was Carlotta's scream."*

WOMAN LIVES IN TERROR OF BIZARRE NIGHTLY ATTACKS
—BY A GHOST! screamed a headline in bold type in the
August 15, 1978, *Midnight/Globe* publication. The article went on to describe the plight of an attractive West
Coast mother of four who had become a victim of nearly
nightly, vicious assaults by a repulsive fiend from another
dimension.

*The Entity, DeFelitta, Frank. Putnam, 1978.

A credible witness to the savagery and brutality of the "entity," told a *Midnight/Globe* reporter, "This is no publicity stunt. She's no jokester. I saw things I cannot explain. . . ."

The witness, none other than noted author, Frank DeFelitta, documented an account of the haunting of Carlotta, entitled, *The Entity*.

"I had to write it as a novel," explained DeFelitta, "because I could not use real names. But it is all based soundly on fact.

"I came to California in 1970, and was confronted by parapsychologists from U.C.L.A. who had heard of my work.

"The same parapsychologists, Barry Taff and Kerry Gaynor, called me three years ago to tell me: 'We are onto something . . . a woman is being taken by a force we cannot pin down.' I went to the woman's house with them.

"The woman was upset at what was happening to her. The attacks were occurring nightly; she was being beaten, bitten, hurt—there were marks all over her body."

DeFelitta consulted a psychiatrist who suggested that the victim perhaps was self-inflicting the injuries and was blaming her wounds on a rapacious ghost. But he was very wrong.

"That night," stated DeFelitta, "I witnessed, personally, something I have never seen. I heard the woman's exhortations, her screams at this thing coming to disturb her . . . and gradually a gaseous, greenish light seemed to take on the form of a muscle, an arm, a shoulder, the back of a neck . . . I was convinced. The most skeptical person on earth would have been convinced."

DeFelitta spent many long months studying the ghostly attacks in an attempt to more accurately understand the nature of the phenomenon. Questions arose. Was the cruel and sadistic deviate really a spirit from the realm of the dead or was it possibly a violent projection of Carlotta's disturbed mind? And could such an image take on visible, physical form?

The victim related to DeFelitta a description of her attacker. He stood nearly seven feet tall, with cruel, oriental features, like a Mongolian barbarian of ancient times. But the creature had the capacity to be tender and loving—when Carlotta cooperated. When it was his pleasure to do so, especially as Carlotta's resistance subsided, the entity rewarded her with inexpressible flights of fantasy and delight. But the price she paid was very high, indeed.

"This thing is killing her," declared DeFelitta. "She is weak and quite possibly ill. At this moment, it's going on. . . ."

Carlotta could feel the ironlike, muscular arms close in around her, holding her body in a vulnerable position, always drawing her nearer. But did the being have physical substance, weight? The victim was not certain. The creature's hands seemed to occupy physical space but the incredible pressure that manipulated her struggling, protesting body was more like gravity—an invisible relentless pressure.

The outraged victim of the "entity" continued to exist for some time in the living horror of that unbelievable recurring nightmare. But, eventually, her mind shattered. And she was drawn, mentally, into another dimension where the creature could have its way with her. Attendants at the mental institution where Carlotta was being treated watched in horrified fascination as darkness approached. Her breathing would come faster, deeper. Suddenly, her serene features would contort into an expression of obvious delight, as she abandoned her lovely young body to the creature. The hospital bed yielded to the incredible violence until Carlotta achieved ultimate satisfaction.

The demon that plagued Carlotta had a nightmarelike quality. The Latin word for nightmare is incubo. And it has been historically associated with male and female agents of demonic lust called incubi and succubi. St. Augustine, an early holy man of Christianity, wrote in his dissertation, *DeCuvitate Dei,* in the fifth century A.D.: "It is widespread belief that sylvans and fauns, commonly called incubi, have frequently molested women." While incubi were busily seeking favors from unsuspecting females, their counterparts, the succubi, preyed upon males, saint and sinner alike, with considerable success.

Albertus Magnus, a German theologian, was elevated to sainthood in 1931. He wrote of these demons: "There are places in which a man can scarcely sleep at night without a succubus accosting him."

The sin of sleeping with a demon is considered a form of bestiality, and is synonymous with sodomy. The penalty for such a sin—eternity in hell, fiery torment and exquisite eternal tortures executed by demons skilled in the art of inflicting perpetual agony.

It is believed by many occultists that a hierarchy of lustful devilish beings exists. For example, female demons called succubi are allegedly under the control of a malevolent arch-demoness named Princess Nahemah. Both incubi and succubi appear to their victims either as night visitors in the flesh or as spirit beings perceived in the form of an erotic dream. Nocturnal emissions have often been attributed to spirits of lust. The chiefs of the hellish hosts directly organize seductions designed to undermine the moral integrity of all men and women, but especially the faithful, or "good" souls. The Devil, himself, is alleged to condone and encourage such encounters.

In ancient times, the interplay between the Devil and his female worshipers was part of the profane witches' sabbath and other obscene ceremonies associated with witchcraft, such as the notorious Black Mass. Both incubi and succubi, according to testimony and written accounts, cavorted wantonly with humankind at coven celebrations. In modern times, self-appointed high priests or priestesses perform initiations of new believers, either symbolically or literally. Many twentieth century covens still claim to be serviced by the Devil and his cohorts.

An account of the Devil giving delightful pleasures of the flesh made headlines in Swiss newspapers as recently as 1966. Bernadette Hasler, a beautiful seventeen-year-old girl, wrote: "I love the Devil. He is beautiful. He visits me nearly every night. He is much better than God. I would like to belong only to the Devil."

Ms. Hasler stated that she had this experience with the Devil a thousand times and maintained steadfast love for her amorous demon until the end. For she died cruelly at the perverse hands of six cultists who attempted to "beat the Devil out of her." Bernadette Hasler was found to be a virgin when she was "executed" for the crime of perversion with the Devil.*

Encounters with insatiable denizens from beyond the grave are not always accounted as pleasurable. Women describe these demonic bodies as cold as ice or painfully huge and made of iron. Sickening sulphuric odors have been reported in connection with ghostly attacks. Men occasionally confirm the unpleasant nature of supernatural succubi. Much of the discomfort could be attributed to, according to the early church, the habit of demons animating the bodies of freshly dead corpses to perform their ghastly assaults. And it was suspected that the cadavers could impregnate mortal females and result in the birth of grotesquely deformed offspring.

The theory that a hierarchy of demons exists that seduces mankind dates back into antiquity. But a more valid explanation for the persistent and alarming reports of sexual ghosts lies within the Bible's mysterious Apocrypha of the Hebrew text. In man's early evolution, according to that ancient account, a race of super beings existed who could take the form of any living creature. They dominated the earth and were incomparably beautiful and intelligent. The Bible refers to the beings as "angels" or "sons of God." But most often, they were called the "Watchers." The Watchers were assigned by the Supreme Being to guide and direct the progress of humanity on earth. As identity evolved, the Watchers took considerable interest in human females. They began taking physical form and openly engaged women.

The unholy union resulted in the creation of monstrous hybrids the Hebrews called Nephilim. The Nephilim were great in size and unprecedented in wickedness. Standing ten feet tall, half man and half god, no man, beast or woman dared resist them. The proliferation of these cruel giants enraged God and prompted the great flood in the days of Noah. Many Nephilim died in that disaster or were forced to withdraw into their spirit form,

---

*Writer, Barbara Conrad is presently fictionalizing a novel based on the life of Bernadette Hasler. A more detailed account is given in the book, *By Lust Possessed*, edited by Eric Lombard and published by Signet, 1980.

never again to be permitted to ravage the human race in an entirely physical body. But some survived and appear again in Hebrew history during the taking of the "promised land." The Hebrews were told to slay the giants on sight and to show no mercy. Archaeologists, however, have found unusually huge skeletons, whole burials, indicating that perhaps many of the Nephilim not only survived but proliferated.

Could the Nephilim and their forefathers still exist as evil spirits and hold an unholy influence over the souls of men and women? Do concepts of devils and demons originate from the reports of wicked deeds committed by the super creatures called Watchers? And did the sexual seduction of females by the Watchers give the human race an unprecedented genetic leap forward in evolution —and the forbidden knowledge of good and evil? Do we owe our dual nature, our inclination to various vices and perversions to the genetic influence of our guardians, the Watchers? And do they still watch, wait and prey upon us? Are the horrid deeds of mass murder such as the Son of Sam killings directly attributed to the whispered encouragement of defiant and rebellious spirit entities? Many religionists think so.

And, according to latest revelations, the bodies of the living can be used by spirits for sensual expression. Jay Barham, the founder of the Church of the Facet of Divinity, has made statements that indicate psychic individuals can be used by unseen forces in a most alarmingly bizarre manner. Barham's church was founded four years ago and is headquartered on a ranchette near renowned psychiatrist, Dr. Elizabeth Kubler-Ross's forty-acre haven for the dying, "Shanti Nilaya," in California. The hospice got its name from a Sanskrit phrase meaning "ultimate home of peace," and is dedicated to the investigation of psychic healing, "life, death and transition." On many occasions, special arrangements have been made for dying patients at Shanti Nilaya to attend Barham's séances. Some who have taken part in his sittings claim entities or spirits, both male and female, sought and received pleasures with them while Rev. Barham and his associates were in an altered trance state.

"Entities," according to reports, have physically materialized in the church's dimly lit séance room and openly solicited favors from sitters. The group believed spirit guides were using energy from Barham and his associates who were lying in deep meditation in a nearby room to manifest physical bodies.

Dr. Kubler-Ross, although not directly associated with Rev. Barham, has maintained belief in his credibility. "He has so much integrity," she has been quoted as saying, and, "the truth does not need to be defended," said the famous scientist. Barham has "healing powers which stun me.

"Poor Kubler-Ross is slipping, has lost her marbles," she said of herself regarding her strong belief in the validity of séance material and life after death. "But I'm convinced that what I am sharing is verifiable. I would not risk my reputation if I were not one hundred percent sure."

The possibility of mankind's spiritual existence after physical death has become a scientific probability in recent years. And, indeed, the ultimate question remains and is yet to be reckoned with, "Is there sex after physical death?" Those living adepts who have successfully freed the fleshly body from the spiritual body (astral projection) maintain having a second, fully equipped form with no change in sexual identity. Astral travelers claim satisfactory encounters on that plain with souls of the living and have attested to a heightened degree of sensual awareness.

In all reported accounts of apparitions being seen by the living, witnesses verify that the physical similarity and the sexual identity remain exactly the same. And, lastly, in all séance material and mediumistic communications, no "dead" soul has ever related or even intimated that his or her sexuality changed after death.

The love feelings that draw male and female together point to a promise of a greater and higher purpose for intimacy than simply physical pleasure or reproduction of the species. Research indicates that spirits have and retain human emotions, can see, and hear—so why would other sensations such as touch be taken away? Ideal sexual pleasure contains an element of unmeasurable bliss, resulting in an altered, heightened state of awareness and oneness not unlike spiritual ecstasy. The unselfish sharing and giving of one another does not stop when men and women mature and can no longer fulfill the act of reproduction. Actually, in most cases, sensual gratification and pleasure intensifies with age, indicating a basic need, other than an instinctive drive to multiply, is being satisfied. It is possible that sensual joy is linked in some way to an unexpected benefit to mankind in the next existence and is symbolic of even a greater union with the Divine Being.

*Full as a crystal cup with drink is my cell with
dreams, and quiet, and cool. . . . Stop, old man!
You must leave a chink: How can I breathe? You
can't you fool!*

Elinor Wylie
(*Sanctuary*)

*"Something was there, standing beside me . . .
an awful presence that could be sensed but not
seen. As soon as I walked down into the basement at Hannah House, I could feel it. I left
the basement when the vibrations intensified
and became uncomfortably strong. . . ."*

Nadine Moore, Librarian
Indianapolis Star

4

The House That Reeks of Death

The great Midwest has often been called the bread basket
of the United States. And justifiably so, for early settlers
left a hardy legacy of strong-minded, God-fearing offspring to till the soil. Perhaps Indianapolis, Indiana, in
the middle of agricultural America, seems an unlikely
spot for a notoriously haunted house—but it does have
one.

The eerie residence is the historic Hannah House, built
in 1858 by Alexander Moore Hannah, a prominent figure
in early Hoosier history. Originally, the twenty-four immense rooms accommodated Hannah and his servants.
When at age fifty-one he married Elizabeth Jackson, he
added a wing to house the help.

When Alexander Hannah built his formidable mansion,
it was a time of great change. In Illinois, Abraham
Lincoln and Stephen A. Douglas were in heated debate
on the question of slavery. Ominous signs of the great
civil strife to come in 1861 were creating a growing unrest
among the people. President James C. Buchanan was
openly in favor of slavery, while many prominent citizens

had already made a defiant stand against it. Alexander Moore Hannah was one of them. Hannah was never a member of any religious organization but gave generously to them all. He was considered a progressive and scientific farmer as well as a humanitarian, and he was respected and admired by the community as a man of conscience. It is easy to understand why Hannah was strongly opposed to slavery.

What causes a fine old mansion such as Hannah House to gain the reputation of being haunted?

Located on Madison Avenue, the stately, red brick, Greek-revival-style giant looms like a leftover from another era. It has been owned by relatively few families, and, unlike many other haunted places, little trauma and hardship has happened there. Hannah owned the home until 1899, when his heirs sold the estate to Roman Oehler. Oehler's daughter, Romena Oehler Elder, later acquired the mansion and it remains in the Elder family at the present time.

Although psychically obtained information is important in determining the reason for a haunting, eye-witnesses can add much insight into the disturbances. Psychic sensitive Lynn Dohrenwend, a local resident, agreed to accompany me to the mansion, which is presently being used for the display and sale of antiques. Meetings were also scheduled with people who had experienced first-hand the numerous hauntings of Hannah House.

An interview with a local professional man who chooses to remain anonymous provided excellent information and added credence to other reports of phenomena occurring in the old structure.

"The Hannah House," he began, "was used as a station in the Underground Railroad link-up prior to the Civil War.

"One of the upstairs rooms sometimes smells like gangrene or decaying flesh. When I first smelled it, I thought it was caused by something like decaying rats between the walls, burning garbage, old food, something like that. But a careful examination revealed nothing. What baffled me was the way the stench would completely disappear one day and return again on another day. It would linger for a few hours, then disappear once again.

"I tried bleach, deodorant, bug spray, perfume, the works—nothing worked. I finally brought in an exterminator service, and even a plumber, who double-checked the pipes—still nothing."

"Do you have any theories to explain the smell?" I asked.

"Only one," he replied. "I said the house used to be part of the Underground Railroad between the South and Canada. The couple who originally owned it kept runaway slaves in the basement. Late at night, they would load the slaves into a horse-drawn wagon and transport them to the next house in the link-up.

"One night a lantern was overturned in the basement, and many of the slaves were trapped in the flames. The fire did extensive damage both to the basement and to the rest of the house. Later, when new owners remodeled, the original basement was covered over."

I felt that this was a plausible theory. In another investigation, I'd learned that rather than risk discovery, runaway slaves who died of wounds or illness were often buried in the cellars of Underground Railroad houses by their would-be benefactors, because a stiff penalty was levied against anyone harboring escaped slaves in those days.

My interest in the old mansion continued to grow. A trip to the library of the *Indianapolis Star* unearthed more of the history of Hannah House, while many newspaper articles provided names of people who had experienced supernatural happenings there.

One such person is Ruth Loux, a parapsychologist and hypnotist who has made many trips to Hannah House, always bringing a recognized psychic practitioner with her.

"We had no difficulty agreeing that we experienced a 'feeling' about one particular room," she said. "After being in the room about fifteen minutes, we heard noises —eerie sounds of moaning and whining, and soon a heavy, sickening odor was detectable. My companion on the investigation complained of a headache, and I became nauseous. It was a smell of flesh, of death, and we went outside for fresh air.

"Upon returning, our hostess took us to the basement, which was free of the dampness usually found in basements. It was here, our guide said, that the slaves had hidden, packed in solid. There was an unmistakable smell of humanity, of sweat. We made five trips to Hannah House in a period of one year, and each time, the sounds and odors in the one room and the basement never changed.

"So many things go on there. Doors that have been locked suddenly open and slam closed by themselves, cold drafts are felt when no windows are open, sounds of footsteps are heard on the stairs, and spoons have been seen lifting from cups and flying through the air."

Mrs. Loux feels that the need to repeat lifetime experiences over and over again after the death transition is an inadequate explanation for ghostly appearances and the seemingly mindless repetition characteristic of their conduct.

"There's got to be something other than simplistic spirit-return happening here." She reached for a nearby volume. "There's one good theory contained in this book," she said. "This author thinks that neither time nor space is actually real and that we all live in a constant 'now.' "

Mrs. Loux began to read: " 'The concept is that everything that has ever happened is happening right now, and that everything that will ever happen in the universe has already happened. In other words, we are all living all our lives, past, present, and future, so to speak, at this moment. There is only a constant 'now.' "*

Ruth Loux's reporting of various phenomena coincided with information from other reliable people who told of supernatural activity at Hannah House.

David Elder, one of the present owners of Hannah House, escorted Lynn Dohrenwend and me through the mansion. Lynn immediately sensed the presence of a strong female figure who had been a domestic in the

---

You Were Born Again To Be Together, by Dick Sutphen.

Hannah household. The woman had strong resentment toward the mistress of the house. Lynn also expressed a feeling that there was a body sealed in the wall of the basement.

After walking through the house and recording psychic impressions, Lynn and I interviewed former occupants Mr. and Mrs. John Francis O'Brien and various members of the Elder family. All were gathered at the house, which had been opened to the public on that particular weekend.

We found Mrs. Gladys O'Brien, the ex-tenant, on the second floor of Hannah House, arranging some antiques.

"How long did you live at Hannah House?" I asked.

She thought for a moment before replying, "My husband and I lived here on and off for about ten years. But the manifestations lasted for four years, from the time we first moved in."

When I asked her to tell me as much as she could remember of the hauntings, her expression suddenly became quite intense. "I've heard the sound of crashing glass at least five times," she said. "And one time two deputy sheriffs were called in, and they both heard the noise.

"When Hannah House was being used as an antique shop, before my husband and I moved in, we were just closing up for the day when I saw a man walking around in the upstairs hall. He was dressed in a black suit. Well, I followed him, because customers weren't allowed to go upstairs alone. But when I got there, I couldn't find him. I decided he must be hiding, for some reason, so I went downstairs and got my husband, my business partner, and her husband. We searched all around but didn't find anyone. I decided I must have hallucinated the whole thing.

"But the most curious thing happened when I hired a painter to do some work for me, and the house rejected him. Pictures fell off the walls and doors closed by themselves when he was around. One day I served him some coffee in the old nursery facing Madison Avenue. I poured the coffee and put the spoon back down on the tray, turned away for a second, and glanced back just in time to see the spoon fly off the tray and hit the wall—all by itself. I tried to convince the painter that it had been caused by the vibrations of a passing truck, but that didn't work. He quit.

"Then my son volunteered to come in after his daytime job and finish painting the house. The first night, he had the distinct impression that something or someone was watching him. That can make you feel pretty uneasy when you're standing on a twelve-foot ladder. The next night, he brought his wife and two little girls along. While he was working, my granddaughter Cheryl was playing on the stairs. Pretty soon he heard her say, 'Hi, Dad.' The grandchildren always called my husband 'Dad.' Well, my son yelled out, 'He's not here!' And she said, 'Oh yes he is.'

"Now, he knew there was no one there, but just to make sure, he asked, 'Well, what's he doing?' Cheryl answered, 'He's rocking in the rocking chair.' My son thought she was playing games. But she kept saying, 'Come on up, Dad, Come on up.' And she kept right on talking to someone he knew wasn't there. This went on for quite some time. Finally, my son got curious and asked, 'What's Dad doing now?' Cheryl answered, 'He's coming up the stairs.' That was too much for everyone. They quit working and left for the night."

"Mrs. O'Brien, did you ever see the man on the stairs?" I asked.

"I've seen a man—I guess it could have been the same person. During a period of time when the strange occurrences had very nearly ceased, two psychics wanted to go through the house. While they were here, I was in the room where the odor is, and in my mind's eye I saw a very elegant-looking old man and heard him say, 'Get downstairs and take care of your own business and leave these damn fool women alone!' "

"Everyone keeps talking about a nauseating odor," I said. "Tell me about your experience with that phenomenon."

"There's a bedroom upstairs that has a very strong smell of rotten flesh. I associate it with gangrene. I'd be working in that room for a short time, and up from the floor would come a terrible smell that would come and go. I scrubbed that floor with carbolic acid, and we even painted it, but the smell persisted, so we just closed the door and used the room for storage. But we had to keep that door closed all the time anyway. Otherwise, we had disturbances out in the hall—doors opening and closing by themselves, strange noises, that sort of thing."

"Weren't you frightened by all that commotion going on in your home?" I asked.

Mrs. O'Brien shrugged. "It bothered me for a long time, but finally I said, 'Look, we're protecting the house and you're scaring the hell out of me.' After that, they didn't bother me too often."

Suddenly Lynn cut in, "I'm picking up psychic impressions of a decomposed body. Also, there's cancer associated with the ghost room. Someone died of cancer there—a woman. And we're talking about different time periods. There's a strong feeling of an aggressive, dominant woman, too."

"You must mean Mr. Hannah's German cook," Mrs. O'Brien replied. "There are people around here who know about the cook, and they've told me she had a very strong, dominant personality, just as you've described. And there was a live-in housekeeper who worked for Mrs. Elder—she died of cancer. But I suggest you talk to my husband—he knows much more about the psychic activity in this house."

While Lynn went in search of Mr. O'Brien, who was somewhere in the house with a customer, I waited by the fireplace. As I ran my fingers along the ornately carved black-walnut woodwork of the mantel, my eyes were caught by a bronze casting in the center of it. A goddess-like woman with beautiful hounds was the subject of the casting, bringing to mind a more gracious era in our country's history. I was studying the hand-carved hounds' heads at each end of the casting, when Lynn returned with John O'Brien in tow.

He flashed me a smile and said, "That's 'Diane and Her Hounds' in bronze. Abraham Lincoln stood in front of it many times during the election year of 1865. He practiced his speeches right where we're standing now. We brought the mantel to Hannah House when the Claypool Hotel was torn down, but it was originally from the Bates home."

"Mr. O'Brien, what were your first impressions of Hannah House when you came here to live?" I asked.

"Well, it didn't take me long to figure out that we had other inhabitants in the house—unseen ones, that is. Every time I'd go into the upstairs rooms, I could tell that something was with me. I could feel it, but I couldn't see a thing. Then, whatever it was would leave me and pick me up again later.

"The house seemed to feel hostile toward my wife and me. We supposed it was because it had been vacant for six years. Vandals had broken in during that time, and we figured that was why the ghostly occupants were stirred up.

"But other unexplainable things kept occurring. I came in one evening and walked across the floor. I took about three steps, and each time my foot touched the floor, it sounded like somebody was underneath, banging the floorboards with a sledgehammer. That happened many times. My wife experienced it too.

"Now, the next room over there," he said, pointing toward an adjoining bedroom, "that room is definitely haunted. The door opens and closes by itself. And I walked in there one morning and it smelled like something or someone had been dead a long time. I tested the floor to see if something had crawled under the boards and died, but I never found a thing. The next instant, the whole atmosphere changed and the room smelled just like a rose garden. I thought maybe there was something wrong with my sense of smell, but my wife also noticed the odor, and so did other people who visited and didn't know a thing about the house."

"Are you saying that the smell just went away, or was it replaced by another smell?"

"It went away all right. Then the room would smell just like a rose garden—like perfume."

"Are there roses growing around here anywhere?" Lynn asked. "I get the impression of lots of roses planted nearby."

"No, we don't have rose bushes. Mrs. Elder, the owner, planted flowers everywhere, but they weren't roses. Or, if she did, they weren't here when we moved in. There are plenty of wild flowers, too, but no roses."

Lynn shook her head. "I still think there were roses planted right near that window," she said, pointing toward the window of the ghost room.

"Other than the strange smells, are there other phenomenal occurrences associated with that room?" I asked.

"The door would open and shut by itself, as I mentioned before. And sometimes when we were watching TV upstairs, I'd hear footsteps loud and clear. When I turned down the set and walked downstairs to the first floor, I could still hear those sounds. And the stairs were carpeted, too. We couldn't hear our own footsteps, but each one of the spirits made different sounds; some would go thump, thump, thump. Then you'd hear light footsteps and clothes rustling. But the noises would stop when I'd get all the way to the bottom of the stairs."

"Did you ever see an entity when you heard the sounds?" I asked.

"I saw an entity on the stairs. There was a man standing in the archway, looking at me. I could see right through him. Before I could say 'boo,' he turned and headed for the hallway. I jumped up off the sofa, to follow him, but he just disappeared. It was definitely a shade or a ghost; it wasn't solid flesh or anything like that. You could actually see through it."

"Could you tell what time period the clothing was from?" Lynn asked.

"Old," he said, his tone very serious. "He had muttonchop sideburns, was medium-sized, and was dressed all in black.

"Things move by themselves here, too," he continued, as he led us into the hallway and over to a narrow attic. "This handle has to be turned in order for the door to shut; otherwise it'll swing open. Well, I heard something upstairs one night, so I ran up here, thinking I'd catch somebody playing tricks. Now, I know I had shut that door, but something must have turned that handle, because it couldn't have opened any other way. That door swung open right in front of my eyes.

"And sometimes there was a loud crashing sound, like a china cabinet falling down—you could hear glass break and wood crunch. You could look all over the house but you wouldn't find anything that tipped over or fell. It didn't happen at regular times, but in the middle of the night or early in the mornings. I think David Elder heard it once."

"Do you think the beings in this house finally accepted you and your wife?" I asked.

Mr. O'Brien nodded. "We could almost see it changing. Instead of the house feeling hostile, it seemed to become friendly. We could actually sense it."

"What seemed to make the biggest change in the nature of the hauntings?"

"I think I can trace it back to one Saturday night when I was watching TV on the second floor. There was no light on in the hallway. Then suddenly I heard this ungodly sound, and it wasn't coming from the TV set. So I turned the sound off and opened the door to the hall. There was definitely someone or something groaning out there. Then it stopped, so I went back to watching TV again. But about an hour later, it started all over again. So I said out loud, 'If I can help you, please tell me. If I can't, then go somewhere else to do your bellyaching.' And the groaning stopped!"

"What's your explanation of the strange things that happened to you and your wife here at Hannah House?" Lynn asked.

"My best guess, and I think my wife would agree, is that the spirits think they're protecting this house."

Mr. O'Brien then introduced us to David Elder's sister, Mrs. Dorothy Elder Gartin.

"What are your early memories of Hannah House? Did you enjoy living here as a child?" I asked her.

"Yes, I did. I liked climbing the trees and running around the yard and exploring the barn. I guess my early years were pretty much like anyone else's. I can't remember anything spooky happening, though."

"What were the illnesses that caused your parents' deaths?" I asked.

"My father died of cancer and my mother died of assorted conditions. But they didn't pass away here—they died at the hospital.

"I keep receiving severe stomach pains, like spasms or cramps," said Lynn. "Someone who once lived here had terrible abdominal cramps. It has something to do with a poisonous substance that was given to a woman who was lying gravely ill in that bedroom." Lynn pointed toward the haunted room. "There's a baby, too—female, I think. It was stillborn to a mature woman. The birth was forced because the infant had made the woman septic. Her system had become poisoned." Lynn looked directly at Mrs. Gartin for confirmation.

"No," she said, shaking her head. "To my knowledge, there was no baby born dead either to my folks or to the Oehlers, who lived here before us. And I don't think the original owners—Mr. Hannah and his wife—had any children either. He was getting along in years when he finally married, and his wife was past the childbearing age. If she did have a baby, no one knows about it."

"I definitely see a pregnant woman, full-term and in severe pain," Lynn insisted. "She was given an herbal substance to induce labor. It all took place in the haunted bedroom."

At this point David Elder joined us.

"David," I began, "Mr. O'Brien told us that you once heard a loud crashing sound at Hannah House."

"I sure did. The house was unoccupied at the time. It had been empty for five years. I was downstairs in the main part of the house, tying up some old newspapers, when there was a loud sound of glass breaking. It seemed to come from the basement. I thought maybe someone had broken in and had knocked over a barrel of fruit jars. But when I ran downstairs, no one was there. I guess it was just a matter of hearing something that wasn't real. But it was a very, very loud sound. Of course, it was a rainy, dreary day, and you can imagine how a noise like that would add to the spooky atmosphere.

"The only other scary thing that I recall is about a piano. My brother Bob told me about an old piano we had at Hannah House when we were kids. He said we'd all be playing in the basement when the piano would start playing by itself. Bob would rush upstairs to check, but the sound would stop before he got to it."

When we left Hannah House, Lynn was tense and silent. Finally she looked at me and said, "There's just *got* to be a child involved with the Hannah couple. It's such a strong impression."

"There's one sure way to find out," I replied. "Let's go to the Crown Hill Cemetery and check the Hannah family plot."

The sun was low in the November sky as we drove into one of Indiana's most historic burial grounds. The guard warned us that we had only a few minutes before closing time, then told us where we'd find the Hannah family plot.

We both stared in amazement, for alongside the tombstones of Alexander and Elizabeth Hannah was a small marker. Apparently the infant had been stillborn or had lived less than one day, for only a single date was chiseled into the marker.

5

No Escape Even in Death

All but the smallest of jails are bedlams. They are permeated with catcalls, mumbling, laughter, crying, swearing, and any other noises that humans can make. Only during the wee hours of the morning is there any semblance of tranquillity.

Sometimes, when a jail is abandoned or converted to another use, the noises continue. Alcatraz is notorious for the strange sounds that come from its upper tiers of cell blocks at night. In the old jail in Tallahassee, the capital of Florida, weird noises originate from unknown sources. From the outside, the old Tallahassee jail doesn't look haunted. Less than fifty years old, the modern white structure, with its gracious architectural lines, looks more like a millionaire's mansion or a library.

The old Tallahassee jail now serves as a repository for the records of Florida's Department of Corrections. Periodically, members of the department staff spend considerable time researching the archives there. Cells that once housed prisoners are now crammed with files and records.

Back in the 1930s, the Tallahassee jail saw more than

45

its share of trauma, violence, redneck justice, and death. Blacks and poor whites endured suffering and hardship there that would frighten even the toughest of modern cons.

When I visited the building in 1979, a number of Correction Department employees were sorting and filing records. I confronted them as a group where they were working in a room off the main cell block. They denied ever having experienced any strange happenings in the old jail.

But, after taking pictures of the cell areas, I returned to the room and talked to several of the workers individually. Two of them, both of whom asked that I not use their names, admitted having heard unusual sounds coming from the cell area when they were working there late at night.

"At first, I thought it might be rats or something. But then I realized that it was too loud for rats, and besides, there are no rats in this building," said one.

The other told how the noises seemed to come from the other side of the door next to which he was working. "As soon as I heard that noise, like someone moving or dragging heavy things, I jerked the door open. But nothing was there. I searched that cell block, but it was empty, and there's no way anyone could get in or out of there without passing me."

I asked them if they had ever seen anything strange or heard noises other than the sounds of people moving about.

"I heard a scream one night that I thought came from the basement," said the first man. "It didn't sound human, but it didn't sound like an animal either. It was quite late, and I was here alone. I was fighting to stay awake. I kept dozing off. But that scream sure woke me up. I left work right away, but I came back the next day."

In the mid-1970s the state of Florida used the jail as a repository for Spanish treasure. The state and the salvagers had a running legal dispute that lasted for several years. The state claimed twenty-five percent of the treasure, which had been recovered from a shipwreck off the

Florida Keys, but the salvagers claimed that the loot was all theirs.* Therefore, the treasure was confiscated by the state and stored in the old jail, awaiting court settlement.

During that time, archaeologists, anthropologists, and other researchers spent a great deal of time examining the artifacts. Untraceable sounds, cold spots, and other phenomena were encountered by the research teams. But these activities were attributed to rats, pigeons, and drafts. The people who experienced them merely shrugged their shoulders and went on with their work. That is, until one of the researchers was virtually thrown down the stairs by someone or something that wasn't there. After that incident, the activities seemed to intensify, causing some concern among the personnel working there.

A woman who was writing a book on the history of the jail was informed of the bizarre occurrences and contacted Patricia Hayes, a leading Florida psychic.

When Pat arrived at Tallahassee, she had no idea why she had been contacted. As soon as she entered the structure, she was overwhelmed by a feeling of evil. She felt as though certain nefarious beings from the spirit world were trying to reach her.

Pat and the authoress scheduled a séance to be held inside the old jail the following night. Pat wanted the archaeologist who had been pushed down the stairs to be present, but right after the incident the man had declared that he would never go back into the building. Pat, who has done psychic research for the books *The Ghost of Flight 401* and *Haunted Houses,* after standing on the stairs down which the scientist had been shoved, said, "There's a lot of hostile energy here. We need that scientist for the séance. I think we'll be able to communicate with the other side through him."

Pat and the writer checked every room and cell in the building. One of the solitary-confinement cells gave off aggressively malevolent vibes. Most of the graffiti on the walls depicted either religion or sex. There was one gruesome sketch of a naked girl with blood spurting from

---

*In 1980, the courts awarded the treasure hunters all of the booty.

where her head should have been. "It was a terrible-looking room," said Pat. "When I walked in it, I felt horrible. It just hung over me like the chills that were coming through. It was an evil chamber. It gave off the worst vibrations I've ever received anywhere. I felt that room would be the best place for the séance. But we needed the archaeologist."

After a considerable amount of persuasion by Pat, the scientist agreed to attend.

The jail teemed with entities, and Pat was able to determine the route most often used by them in their haunting. At first she wasn't sure whether the spirits were associated with the valuable treasure that had been kept there or with the prisoners who had been incarcerated within the walls. She would find out, to everyone's surprise, that the most evil haunter in the place had never served time there, nor had he anything to do with the Spanish treasure. "I felt that the archaeologist was probably pushed down the stairs because he happened to be on the steps when the entities were passing," said Pat.

That night, five persons—Pat, the writer, the archaeologist, another scientist, and a friend of the writer—gathered in the third-floor solitary-confinement cell. Their only source of light was flashlights that they had brought with them.

Pat said, "I got the worst feelings and vibrations ever. I knew that it wasn't just me—I could see that the others were frightened too. I learned later that two black men had escaped from that cell but were later caught and hanged by a posse in the middle of the night.

"We were sitting in there on old crates holding hands. I could tell the others were beginning to get bored. Suddenly the writer jumped up and landed practically in my lap. She had felt something pulling or tugging on her sleeve. The person who was holding my left hand suddenly started squeezing it very hard. The room got cold. The entities that we couldn't reach on vibrations of love were beginning to come through on vibrations of fear. Our séance was under way, and information was coming through to different people. Most of the communication was through the archaeologist who had been pushed down the stairs. The spirit told us, through him, that four or five feet away from the incinerator was a false wall and beyond it a false door. Under the floor there would be a knife and two beer bottles.

"One of the spirits who came through had once been in a position of authority at the jail, maybe a guard. He was a very evil character and often abused the prisoners. He was coming in strong. I could visualize him. He seemed about to materialize. The vibes were laced with evil and were getting worse. I've been doing this kind of work for eighteen years and never before had I felt such malevolence. I knew we had to get out of there or the situation would get completely out of hand. The feeling of evil was so strong, it was terrible. I don't know if it was panic or what, but without giving it any further thought, I broke off the séance.

"I wanted to get out of that building right away, but the archaeologist said that he was curious to see if there really was a secret room. It was already nine-thirty at night, but we decided to stay.

"About a half hour later, the archaeologist broke through the wall about five feet to the left of the incinerator. He chopped out a hole large enough to crawl through, and then entered it. We waited anxiously, and about fifteen minutes later he emerged, his hair full of white dust. He was holding a knife and two brown beer bottles. It was very evidential, because the entities had told us where to find the secret room and false floor. It was important evidence in proving life after death."

The next day, Pat tuned back into her psychic state of the previous night. Taking out a sheet of paper, she began to sketch a picture of the malevolent spirit who had attempted to materialize during the séance.

The picture, which was mostly in pastels, was shown to some individuals who had been associated with the building when it was still being used as a jail. They immediately recognized the picture as that of a man who had been affiliated with the jail. "He wasn't exactly a guard," said Pat, "but he used to pick up vagrants and other indigent persons and put them to work as slave laborers on farms or road gangs. He was a cruel, mean man. His name was Harvey or something like that. Psychically, he is one of the ugliest personalities I've ever met. He was probably like that in life, which could be the reason for his having been murdered. If given a chance, he can control living persons with negative vibrations. He can take possession of them, and he has already done a lot of damage in influencing the living."

* * *

Carrollton is the seat of Pickens County, Alabama. Carrollton is a nostalgic, picturesque town, not much different in appearance from what it was a hundred years ago. Sometimes, though, it is not a very cheerful place, for when the sky is overcast, "they" appear, and nothing can be done about it.

A judge, a sheriff, a reverend, and others have attested to the apparitional phenomena that take place at the Pickens County Courthouse. "They're from another world," said one official.

Ever since the courthouse was built in 1876, after the first one burned down, a face has appeared on one of its attic windows. The apparition, which has been seen by hundreds of people, is believed to be the ghost of Sam Burhalter, who was run down and killed by a posse many years ago after he burned down the previous county courthouse. Burhalter's face seems troubled and full of pain.

Then, one day, there appeared a second face on the courthouse window. It is that of Lee Summerville, a black man who was shot to death by a Sumter County deputy at York, Alabama, while being sought in connection with the murder of a deputy sheriff.

Both men's faces are seen in the window from a distance of several hundred feet but not from closer or farther away. And, on overcast days, they move about on the glass pane.

In 1968, a carpenter removed the haunted window and replaced it with a new sheet of glass. The ghostly reflections still appeared. The images do not indicate whether the faces are white or black; they are only studies of expression.

"These pictures are not hallucinations. Anyone who cares to do so may see them at any time, just as many hundreds of people have seen them in the past," said a local judge.

* * *

As Mary Surratt said to the priest who was accompanying her while she was being led to the gallows for her part in the conspiracy to assassinate President Abraham Lincoln, "Father, I have something to say—I am innocent!"

The testimonies of two witnesses, one a known liar and the other a notorious drunk, were instrumental in Mrs. Surratt's conviction. She and three other defendants were sentenced to be "hanged by the neck until dead." She was the last of the four to be hanged on July 7, 1865.

The board that conducted the trial and found Mary Surratt guilty had sent a petition to President Johnson asking that her sentence be commuted to life in prison. Whether it was because she was a woman or because they had some doubts about her guilt is unknown. The commander of the federal troops stationed in Washington was so sure that a last-minute reprieve would come from the president that he ordered messengers on horseback stationed along the shortest route between the White House and the Washington Arsenal Prison, where the execution was scheduled to take place.

Right up until the white hood was placed over her head, Mrs. Surratt was sure that she would be spared. While she and three others died that day, another three defendants, including the legendary Dr. Samuel Mudd, received long prison sentences. Mrs. Surratt's son, who fled to Canada, was later returned for trial but was acquitted. And John Wilkes Booth, the actual assassin, died in a barn either by his own hand or by a bullet from a soldier's gun, near Fredericksburg, Virginia. To this day, many historians believe that Mary Surratt and some of her codefendants were innocent.

Mary Surratt may be dead, but she is not gone. The Washington Arsenal Prison has been converted to what is now Fort Leslie J. McNair. The courthouse in which Mary was tried, found guilty, and sentenced is now an officers' quarters at the army base. The actual courtroom in which the history-making trial took place is now a five-room apartment occupied by a lieutenant, his wife, their three-year-old son, and their German shepherd dog.

"There's something bizarre going on here," said the lieutenant. He told of how he and his family have felt the eerie presence of a ghost. He and a neighbor have seen an apparition of a stout, middle-aged woman, dressed in black, seemingly floating through the hallways of the officers' quarters. Strange sounds and unexplainable voices are heard. And the sensation of being touched by an unseen hand is not uncommon there.

The first haunting occurred in 1977, just after he and his wife moved into the 190-year-old building. "We were awakened in the middle of the night by what sounded like murmuring voices," his wife said. "They seemed to be coming from every direction at once."

The baby woke up screaming one night while his parents were in the living room watching TV. The lieutenant went into the bedroom to try to soothe him. But his efforts were futile. Then when the young officer felt what he thought was his wife's hand on his shoulder, the baby fell asleep immediately.

When he returned to the living room, his wife was already back there. "You really have a magic touch. The baby fell asleep just as you put your hand on my shoulder," he said.

"I wasn't in the bedroom," replied the startled mother. "I've been here watching TV the whole time."

On another occasion they heard chains rattling somewhere behind the baby's crib. Their dog wears a heavy chain collar, and they thought it was the dog scratching. That is, until they found the animal sound asleep in another room. The seven male defendants at the conspiracy trial were shackled with chains and sat on a bench near where the baby's crib was located.

During the summer of 1978, the lieutenant was standing in the hallway at about 2:00 A.M. when he saw what he thought was his wife leaving the bedroom and going into the bathroom. But when he went into the bedroom, his wife was in bed, sound asleep. He rushed into the bathroom, but there was no one there.

An Army major's wife in the next apartment has also

seen the woman in a long, dark dress floating around. She knew the history of the building and the trial that took place there. "It was Mary Surratt," she said.

Does the ghost of Mary Surratt stay in that building in which she was sentenced to death, to proclaim her innocence? If not, why does her spirit prowl the premises?

* * *

Almost two years before Mary Surratt was executed, Chipita Rodriguez was hanged. It is said that now, whenever a woman faces the death sentence in Texas, the spirit of Chipita Rodriguez paces the banks of the Nueces River not far from the town of San Patricio.

San Patricio was founded in 1830 by a group of Irish immigrants under the leadership of John McMullen and James McGloin. For many years, Gaelic was the language of that remote Texas town. San Patricio did not appear to be the frontier town that it was, for most of the men dressed in top hats and Prince Albert coats, the women wore silk, and it was not unusual for families to sit down for dinner in full evening dress.

Located some twenty-five miles upstream from Corpus Christi Bay, San Patricio was the site of a key battle in the Texas Revolution. The fight, which occurred only a few days before the siege of the Alamo, was a victory for the Mexicans. During the years of the Texas Republic and into the transition to statehood, San Patricio boomed. Houses and cabins sprang up everywhere. A wooden courthouse was erected with a small lean-to at the rear which served as a jail. The surrounding area was the scene of a continuing feud between law-abiding citizens and renegade bands of Indians and outlaws.

During the Civil War, when cotton was the South's chief trading commodity, cotton-laden wagons often rumbled through San Patricio en route to blockade-running ships off the Texas coast, or on to Mexico, where the cotton was loaded aboard Europe-bound vessels after the blockade of Texas was tightened. This was known as "the Cotton Road" and San Patricio was a key point along it.

For a number of years before the Civil War, Chipita

Rodriguez ran a small log-cabin inn alongside the Arkansas River a few miles from San Patricio. Her clientele consisted mostly of trail riders in search of food and lodging. Chipita, whose real name was Josephina, was the daughter of a Mexican who fled to Texas to join the fight against Santa Anna, the Mexican dictator; her father was killed during Texas' fight for freedom. After living alone for a number of years, she took up with a cowboy and soon bore him a son.

Then one day the cowboy left her, taking their son with him. Loneliness and a broken heart forced her to leave her place on the Arkansas River for a location closer to town. Her new inn became a hangout for gamblers and cowboys. In spite of all the activity, Chipita was forlorn and lonely.

In 1863, during the height of the Civil War, a horse trader named John Savage rode up to Chipita's place with five hundred pieces of gold in his saddlebags. He paid for a night's lodging and sat down to dinner. While Chipita was preparing the meal, she glanced out the window. She was so startled that she dropped the soup ladle she was holding. It was her old lover—the father of her son. But then she realized that the stranger was too young, for she herself was already middle-aged.

The stranger paid for his bed and went to sleep without eating. He looked so familiar to Chipita that she lay awake for several hours wondering about him.

Shortly before daybreak, a scream resounded through the main building where the two travelers were sleeping. Chipita, wrapping herself in a blanket, ran from her hut to the big cabin. No one was there. When she walked out on the other side, she found the bloody body of John Savage, murdered. He had been slaughtered with an ax that Chipita used to cut firewood. His saddlebags with the gold were gone. She heard the distant sound of hoofbeats and looked up just in time to see the stranger riding off for parts unknown.

Chipita was brought to San Patricio for questioning and was then charged with the murder of John Savage. Another man, Ivan Silvera, who was a part-time hired hand at Chipita's place, was charged as her accomplice.

While awaiting trial, they were kept chained to the walls of separate cells in the lean-to jail at the rear of the Fourteenth District Courthouse in San Patricio.

As federal troops were spreading across Texas in the fall of 1863, Silvera went to trial. He was found guilty of second-degree murder and sentenced to six years in the penitentiary.

Except for pleading "not guilty," Chipita maintained silence throughout the trial. The jury found her guilty of murder in the first degree; however, because of her age and the fact that evidence against her was circumstantial at best, they recommended mercy. But there would be no mercy.

Judge Benjamin F. Neal ordered Chipita Rodriguez to be confined until sunset on Friday, the thirteenth of November, 1963, and at that time to be "hanged by the neck until dead."

So, as Northern troops were driving toward San Patricio, Chipita was taken from the lean-to jail to a lone mesquite tree on the bank of the Nueces River, where she was hanged. Her body was then dropped into a plain board coffin and placed in an unmarked grave.

As Chipita sat chained in jail awaiting her date with the hangman, she had a number of sympathetic visitors who brought her food, tobacco and drink. One of those was Mrs. Kate McCumber, the only person to whom Chipita told the true story of the murder of John Savage. Mrs. McCumber was sworn to secrecy until after the hanging.

After Chipita's coffin was dumped unceremoniously into a shallow grave, the story was let out: The stranger who bore such a marked likeness to her long-gone lover was the killer of John Savage; he was also Chipita's long-lost son.

During the last 117 years, an apparition bearing similar appearance to Chipita has been seen along the banks of the Nueces whenever a woman sits on death row in Texas. Sometimes she appears as no more than a shadow. On other occasions, she has been seen under a full moon with a hangman's noose around her neck. Still other accounts tell of her materialization being surrounded by a mysterious, auralike glow. Most often, however, only her sobbing cries are heard. But, whatever form she takes, there have been enough sightings reported to justify the hauntings as more than just folklore or legend.

*Hampton's mystique involves a mystifying chan-
delier, a haunted tack room, ten gabled bedrooms, a circular stairway leading to an eerie-
looking cupola that straddles the roof like an
architectural specter, and, of course, many
ghosts.*

6

Crashing Chandeliers and Death

Hampton Mansion, ten miles north of Baltimore, is both
charming and impressive in the daylight, its monstrous
proportions dominating the forty-acre tract on which it
sits. The post–Revolutionary War giant appears serene
among the cedar, catalpa, and magnolia trees that artfully
frame it like a well-preserved portrait of another era. But
when the gray mist of evening begins to swirl ominously
around the immense three-story strucure, a new personality emerges. Strange, grotesque shadows flit men-
acingly around shrubs and trees that seem harmless in the
sunlight. As the magic of night transforms its character,
the haunters of Hampton are once again its masters,
prowling the dark hallways and grounds.

Hampton was built for Captain Charles Ridgely and
his descendants, who occupied it for over 150 years. Its
builder, Jehu Howell, a local carpenter, was probably its
architect too. According to the Ridgely family records,
the handsome payment he received for his work included
sixty-eight quarts of rum.

Howell did not survive to enjoy his financial windfall,
however. Jehu Howell drowned in November 1787, when

"he permitted his horse to enter the water, at the end of the Ferry-Point, supposing it shallow—but alas! He was fatally mistaken." Perhaps Jehu Howell had taken one too many drinks of Ridgely rum. The *Maryland Journal* and the *Baltimore Advertiser* eulogized Howell as "a very ingenious architect." And indeed he was, for Hampton looks more like a state capitol building than an American manor house. Today, it appears quite the same as it did when Howell built it around 1783.

The Ridgely family occupied the mansion until 1948, when the Avalon Foundation, a philanthropic organization, procured Hampton and gave it to the federal government. The Society for the Preservation of Maryland Antiquities acts as custodian. Hampton is now a National Historic Site and as such is operated by the National Park Service and is open to the public.

Duncan H. Mackenzie, executive director of the Society for the Preservation of Maryland Antiquities, maintains an office in the stately mansion and served as our host at Hampton. Mr. Mackenzie, one of Maryland's finest historians, began with the history of the hauntings.

"Priscilla Dorsey Ridgely, once the mistress of Hampton and wife of Governor Ridgely, converted to Methodism. While the governor entertained his boisterous drinking friends on the lower level, Priscilla would have prayer meetings upstairs.

"In spite of her orthodox religious beliefs, Priscilla bore eleven children at Hampton. Yet, she was never truly happy. Neither her large family, her great wealth, nor her religion afforded her peace of mind. Family members and servants, as well as those sensitive to the supernatural, have seen the melancholy spirit of Mrs. Ridgely, shadowlike in a plain gray gown, wandering aimlessly about the premises.

"When the Ridgely family still occupied Hampton, a new bride in the family opened the door one cool, misty night to find a frail woman standing on the front stoop. The woman appeared distressed and was invited by the mistress of Hampton to come in and warm herself by the fire. But the thin, frail woman raised her eyes pleadingly to the young bride, then turned away abruptly, and vanished like a vapor among the trees.

"Hampton also has haunted chandeliers. A lady who went to Hampton was shown around the manor by a formally attired black butler. The butler advised her that the owners were not at home but that no one knew the old manor better than he, and he proceeded to escort her on a guided tour of Hampton. When the visitor attempted to thank the Ridgelys later for their hospitality in absentia, she was informed that no one had been at the mansion the day of her mysterious tour. She was further advised that the servant she described who had shown her around Hampton had been dead for generations. The visitor was indignant.

" 'Please believe me,' she pleaded. 'It is impossible for that gentleman to be a ghost, for he appeared to me as solid flesh and told me many secrets about the house, including the story of the haunted chandeliers. Your butler told me, 'No matter how good the health of any first lady of Hampton seems to be, those glass lights know when the hour of her death is near, and they come crashing down. Every soul at Hampton hears the noise. The glass smashes up into a thousand little pieces, but when we come running, they're all back in place again. But a day or two later, the lady of Hampton falls dead. I've seen it happen in my time—yes indeed. I wish they weren't there anymore; little death bells, they are—little death bells.' '

"And it was true, for it had happened on many occasions. It always heralded the death of a first lady of Hampton. The fifth mistress of Hampton sat with her family gathered about her one Easter day. They heard a loud crash and the shattering of glass resounded through the great hall. The children and the housekeeper, Lena Bevan, rushed to the room where the crash had been heard. But there was no broken chandelier there, nor anywhere else in the house. Within twenty-four hours, that Mrs. Ridgely died.

"When Mr. Charles, master of Hampton, died in Rome of the fever, tinkling sleigh bells and the sounds of horses' hooves were heard rounding the drive in the dead of a snowy winter night. Even before the telegram was received, telling of Mr. Charles's untimely death, the Ridgely household was already in deep mourning. And it had always been so—when the master of Hampton died, away from home, his soul was gathered back home by a spectral coach. The caretakers at Hampton and the Ridgelys' liveryman both heard the ghostly sleigh that cold winter night.

"Of course, we always hear latches being lifted, bolts being drawn and withdrawn, and doors open by themselves here at Hampton. But there's never a theft, and nothing has been disturbed. And no one has ever been discovered prowling about the premises.

"The 'ghost room' is the northwest bedroom," Mr. Mackenzie continued. "It got its name because Governor Swann's daughter 'Cygnet' died there. She was a lovely young thing, a fair-skinned beauty with long golden hair. 'Cygnet' was a nickname, meaning 'little swan,' given to her by Eliza Ridgely. Cygnet, who was very much loved by the Ridgely family, died suddenly after having a premonitive dream of death. That very morning she shared her nightmare with members of the family. Everyone assured her that such an evil dream could never come true. But, on the eve of a gala ball at Hampton in Cygnet's honor, as she sat brushing her blond hair in front of a vanity mirror, the angel of death came. Cygnet was found slumped forward in front of her vanity, a hairbrush grasped tightly in her hand. Hundreds of people have claimed to have seen Cygnet, dressed in a satin ball gown, sitting silently in the 'ghost room,' brushing her long blond hair."

I followed Mr. Mackenzie down a hallway and into a spacious combination bedroom and sitting room. It was furnished exactly as it might have been when the beautiful Cygnet died there in the 1800s. The floor was covered with a fine Turkish rug, and a portrait of Mrs. Charles Ridgely hung over the mantel. A large four-poster bed, with delicate carvings and hand-blocked English chintz quilted bedspread, added to the mood of the room. A Récamier French-style sofa, a secretary, and miscellaneous appointments—all period pieces—filled the room.

Muted rays of sunlight filtered through cream-colored curtains.

Mr. Mackenzie stood in the doorway with a skeptic's grin on his face as I walked around the room, picking up vibrations and impressions. There was a strong emanation of energy centered near the desk.

"Mr. Mackenzie," I said, "I'd like you to help me with an experiment. Just walk around the room with your palms down until you find an area that impresses you as having a different feeling."

The vibration around the desk was so strong that he sensed it immediately, and, with surprise in his voice, he said "You're right! It's here!" Standing over the desk chair with his arms outstretched, palms down he continued, "I don't know what it is, but I get a prickly sensation in my palms, and it's strong."

Mr. Mackenzie then suggested that I speak with one of the National Park Service rangers who work at Hampton, and escorted me to an office complex located in the basement.

After Mr. Mackenzie made the introductions, I asked the ranger if he had ever had any unusual experiences while working there.

"Some pretty strange things happen here," he answered. "And one of the most unusual experiences I've ever had since I entered the Park Service happened right here in this house one morning—about five-thirty, in January 1977. Another ranger and I heard footsteps out in the hall. They were very, very distinct. I opened the door and ran out into the hallway. Believe me, I searched all around, but there was nothing.

"Two nights later, on Saturday, we had been watching television and had just turned off the set before going to bed. Suddenly I heard all this noise from the room right next to us. It was very loud and there was no doubt that something was going on. At first it sounded like someone was beating chains against the wall.

"We both got up, thinking maybe an intruder had hidden away with the idea of staying overnight, or maybe a thief was breaking in. We didn't know what was out there, so we got our weapons. After a few moments of hesitation, we went into the next room prepared for anything. There was a good deal of tack equipment— harnesses, saddles, that sort of thing—hanging from pegs on the walls. The stuff had been hanging there for years and years. When we walked into the room, everything was swaying back and forth rather violently. And it wasn't a windy night or anything like that. Also, the windows and doors were securely closed.

"After we found all that going on, we thought we'd better check out the rest of the house. We started in the basement and worked our way up. When we got to the great hall where protective bars cover the tops of the doors and the windows—well, the bars on the door facing the garden side of the house had been torn down. We didn't know what to make of it. But there is a Ridgely family legend that tells of those bars flying down by themselves for no reason."

The ranger pointed toward the staircase and continued, "Every once in a while, someone, visitors and staff alike, will hear harpsichord music coming from the ghost room. But there's no harpsichord in the building. And, to my knowledge, several persons, including one of the secretaries, have seen apparitions. But they can't identify any of them. However, there has been some speculation that Jehu Howell, Hampton's builder, who drowned with his horse, may be the haunter of the tack room."

I was also told of one occasion when the great hall at Hampton had been used for an exhibition. During the night, the ranger on guard duty was awakened by a resounding crash. He charged into the great hall to find all the display racks knocked to the floor. There was no explanation for the occurrence. He surmised that the ghosts of Hampton disliked the great hall being used for such mundane purposes.

A little distance from the prow
Those crimson shadows were;
I turned my eyes upon the deck—
O Christ! what I saw there!
    Samuel Taylor Coleridge
    (*Rime of the Ancient Mariner*)

7

Ghosts of the Sea

Probably the most famous of all maritime hauntings was that of the *Leviathan,* one of the most jinxed vessels ever to put to sea. She experienced nearly every calamity except sinking. Not until the ship was being dismantled, nearly forty years after being launched, was it discovered that during her entire oceangoing life she had been haunted by a pair of very unhappy ghosts.

The keel of the seven-hundred-foot *Leviathan* was laid alongside the Thames River in May 1854. Between then and the time construction was completed three years later, an almost endless array of shipyard tragedies befell the twenty-two-thousand-ton vessel. Men fell from scaffolding; workers were decapitated; many had their heads split open by falling objects; some, especially the child laborers not yet in their teens, died from overwork; a few workers even vanished deep within the bowels of the great ship. No one knows exactly how many of the two thousand men who toiled to build the *Leviathan* met death on the job, but the number is said to be in the hundreds.

On November 3, 1857, Miss Hope, daughter of the

owner of the accursed and infamous Hope diamond, smashed a bottle of wine against the *Leviathan*'s bow, signaling its launching. Wedges were knocked loose, chains were released, and, with the help of hydraulic rams, the giant hull slid sideways toward the water.

The vessel moved only six feet, then stopped—jammed at a precarious angle. A shipyard worker was smashed to a pulp during that attempt. Two others drowned when they jumped into the water to escape the flailing arms of a capstan winch whose gears had been stripped. Another dozen workers were injured, five of them seriously, during the ill-attempted launch.

Three weeks later, another launch was attempted. On that day over a hundred spectators were injured when a reviewing stand collapsed. The ship did not move at all that day.

Finally, after weeks of unceasing effort and with the help of more than two hundred workers, the *Leviathan* slid into the water on January 31, 1858. However, on that day the owners, Eastern Steam Navigation Company, went bankrupt.

A new financial syndicate, the Great Ship Company, was organized to finish outfitting the floating colossus, which had been lying idle at her dock. The new organization renamed the vessel the *Great Eastern*.

On September 9, 1859, the day the ship was scheduled for her shakedown cruise, her designer, Isambard Kingdom Brunel, suffered a fatal stroke while standing on deck posing for photographs.

After Brunel was carried ashore, the *Great Eastern* steamed into the Thames. Suddenly the world's then-largest vessel was rocked by an explosion. A steam exhaust valve had been left shut. Firemen were scalded to death. Another crewman was fatally mangled when he was swept under a paddlewheel after jumping overboard to escape the explosion. That same day, a number of persons aboard the ship reported hearing violent pounding that seemed to originate deep in the bowels of the vessel. A search led by the captain, William Harrison, disclosed no source for the sound. The following day, a fireman in one of the boiler rooms had his hand severed when his shirt sleeve became entangled in a steam pipe.

During that same month there was an attempted mutiny aboard the *Great Eastern*. The violence that erupted was so great that almost half the crew had to be confined or placed in irons.

On January 21, 1860, tragedy again struck the *Great Eastern*. One of her boats was being rowed ashore by several of the crew. Aboard were Captain Harrison, one of the ship's mates, and a nine-year-old boy. The boat capsized, and Harrison and the boy drowned.

At that time, the *Great Eastern* was considered the safest ship ever built. She was faster and larger than anything else afloat. She was built with a double bottom —one hull within another—with thirty-four inches between hulls. She set forth on her maiden voyage on June 17, 1860, three years after she was completed. Her destination was New York. She had a crew of four hundred and accommodations for four thousand passengers. However, there were only thirty-six passengers on the *Great Eastern*'s first trans-Atlantic crossing. Financially, the first voyage was a disaster.

The vessel had six towering masts. On her first day at sea en route to New York, it was decided to test her sails. After six hours of enormous effort, the sails were finally hoisted and set and the engines were shut off. The *Great Eastern* stopped. The ratio of the sail area to the ship's weight had been grossly miscalculated. The ship could not sail.

When the sails were lowered, the steam throttle valves to the main engines were opened. Within minutes the engines faltered and stopped.

After three days of wallowing helplessly in the North Atlantic while the machinery was being repaired, the *Great Eastern* finally got under way. During the voyage the captain received reports from various members of the crew concerning strange hammering noises coming from somewhere near the bottom of the ship. No source for the mysterious sounds could be found.

Three days before the ship was due to arrive in New York, a berserk seaman armed with a meat cleaver had to be subdued by several passengers and crewmen.

Among the thousands waiting at New York harbor to welcome the *Great Eastern* after her eleven-day trans-

Atlantic voyage were the occupants of a small boat approaching Bedloe's Island. They were a U.S. marshal, a priest, an executioner, and a condemned man. The execution had been delayed long enough to permit Albert Hicks, the last man to be executed for piracy in the United States, to see the fanfare. The last thing Hicks saw before the executioner placed the hood over his head was the *Great Eastern* steaming into the harbor.

As the *Great Eastern* was docking, she struck the wharf and badly damaged one of her paddlewheels. The first five feet of the wooden pier were ground to splinters.

When customs inspectors heard strange sounds coming from deep inside the ship, they had to be convinced that no stowaways were aboard.

Two of the ship's stokers, drunk on beer, returned to the ship to report for duty, only to fall overboard and drown.

A fire broke out on the dock alongside the *Great Eastern.* Two different fire departments arrived at the same time—the New York City Fire Department, and the Harbor Fire Department. A fight broke out between the two fire departments over who had the right to put out the fire. Five firemen were shot, three were axed, and others were clubbed. The fire was put out by the ship's crew.

On her return to England, the *Great Eastern* collided with the frigate *Blenheim,* nearly sinking the latter.

In September 1861, the great ship set out on her second voyage to New York, with four hundred passengers aboard. However, she got only as far as the Irish Sea, where she encountered a gale. One paddlewheel was completely torn away, and the other was damaged beyond repair. Four lifeboats were washed away, and the steering mechanism was rendered useless.

Although there were no fatalities, 130 passengers were injured. While the ship was limping back to port, a group of off-duty stokers broke into the liquor stores, got drunk, and mutinied. Male passengers were issued arms to subdue the mutineers.

With a jury-rigged rudder, the *Great Eastern* finally made her way back to port, using her huge propeller, which was even larger in diameter than the one in the present-day *Queen Mary*.

As the passengers disembarked, vowing never to set foot aboard the ship again, several complained of strange noises coming from far below the deck.

Only the ship's double bottom saved her from sinking. Workmen, toiling for weeks to repair the vessel reported strange pounding noises coming from within the *Great Eastern*'s double bottom. Walter Patten, the captain, scoffed at the reports until he himself heard the noises. His investigation revealed a loose swivel, which was promptly secured. However, the pounding continued.

When the *Great Eastern* finally did reach New York for the second time, she struck a submerged rock in Long Island Sound, ripping an eighty-three-foot gash in her outer hull. The rock, which is twenty-four feet beneath the surface, is still referred to as "Great Eastern Rock" on nautical charts of the area.

While repairs were being made in New York, American workmen also were disturbed by the weird pounding noises emanating from far down in the ship's hull. Again, the sounds were attributed to a loose swivel. But no loose swivel could be found.

In December 1863, the owners went bankrupt, and the *Great Eastern* was sold at public auction for a paltry $125,000. Converted into a cable-laying ship, the *Great Eastern* commenced laying the first trans-Atlantic cable. But the jinx still hounded the ship. After laying 1,240 miles of cable without incident, the ship failed to stop in time for one of the splicing operations, and the end of the cable slipped over the stern and disappeared forever.

After years of bitter frustration and ridicule, success came to the great ship, for on July 27, 1866, the *Great Eastern* succeeded in laying the first trans-Atlantic communications cable. But her success and glory were short-lived.

Her last voyage as a passenger ship took place in 1867, when she was chartered by a French company. She sailed from New York to France on a special excursion voyage for the Paris Exposition. Only 190 passengers were aboard. Among them was Jules Verne, the great science-

fiction writer. Verne used the *Great Eastern* as the model
for the supership in his fantastic novel *The Floating
City*.

Many who were on that voyage said that a number of
the grisly events in Verne's book actually occurred
aboard the *Great Eastern*. One in particular—the failure
of an anchor winch—caused the capstan bars to flail
around wildly, out of control. That incident sent seven-
ty-six sailors flying and decapitated no less than four of
them. Within months, the French company went bankrupt.

Jinxes and hard luck continued to plague the *Great
Eastern* until November 1888, at which time it was decided to scrap the world's largest ship. Even during the
dismantling, the wrecking crews could hear strange hammering sounds coming from between the ship's double
bottom.

It took almost two years for the wrecking crews to
demolish the great iron ship down to her double bottom.
Late in the summer of 1890, the wreckers penetrated the
three-foot section between the inner and outer hulls. As
the bottom plates were knocked off section by section,
tools that had been left in the hull by workers who had
built her nearly forty years before were found scattered
throughout the double bottom. At night, after the wrecking crews had gone home, watchmen reported pounding
noises coming from what was left of the nearly dismantled
ship.

The wreckers worked on. Then they made a discovery
that was so horrible that further dismantling of the ship
was suspended for several days. The grisly discovery
solved a number of the mysterious happenings that had
plagued the *Great Eastern* throughout her career. But, at
the same time, it made them even more bizarre. The
wreckers found the skeletal remains of two riveters, a
man and his boy apprentice who had vanished thirty-six
years before, while working on the construction of the
ship. It appeared that they had inadvertently been sealed
in between the hulls by fellow workers, who couldn't hear
their screams and pounding because of the noise being
made by other workmen. The periodic pounding from

deep in the ship's hull was attributed to the ghosts of the two entombed riveters.

Although it was several more months before the ship was completely dismantled, no more accidents occurred on the job, nor was the hammering from her double bottom ever heard again after the removal of the skeletons.

One of the most famous nautical haunters is a Tasmanian adventurer who emigrated to the United States, where he made and lost a fortune. Errol Leslie Thomson Flynn, better known as Errol Flynn, always owned a yacht after his climb to stardom. There has been much controversy as to whether his yachts were used for fulfilling his lust for the sea or his lust for young women. Some of the wildest seagoing parties ever given were held aboard Flynn's yacht *Sirocco*.

During World War II, Flynn, the Hollywood "he-man," somehow managed to avoid military service. While American sailors were sacrificing their lives in the Pacific, Errol Flynn was also sailing the Pacific—between Los Angeles and Catalina, hosting orgies aboard the *Sirocco*. It has been said that he bought his way out of the service. In real life, he was far from being the hero that he portrayed on the screen. Unlike other celebrities, Flynn never offered to entertain American servicemen, and he is said to have sold U.S. military information to both Nazi Germany and Japan.

After the war, the *Sirocco* was sold. Flynn replaced it with a 118-foot, two-masted schooner named *Zaca,* which is Samoan for "peace." Just as *Sirocco* was best known for Flynn's drunken parties, *Zaca* soon became famous as the place where he seduced teenaged girls, for which he was arrested on a number of occasions.

Many famous movie stars, including John Barrymore, Alan Hale, David Niven, and Gary Cooper, had been guests aboard the *Zaca*. Flynn and Nora Eddington, the second of his three wives, spent their happiest moments aboard the schooner—until Nora discovered how many other women were also spending their happiest moments on the vessel.

Other celebrities, such as Mary Pickford and Ali Khan, had chartered the *Zaca*. Flynn's guests were often entertained by fights between him and various members of the crew. On one occasion, after a crewman engaged in a fight with the captain, the star picked up the luckless sailor and threw him overboard.

Flynn spent the last happy moments of his life aboard the *Zaca* with sixteen-year-old Beverly Aadland, the last of his many loves. Toward the end, Flynn, quite ill and in dire financial straits, moved the *Zaca* up the coast from Los Angeles to Vancouver to prevent it from falling into the hands of the Internal Revenue Service.

Badly in need of money, Flynn decided that the *Zaca* should be sold. On October 14, 1959, a Vancouver couple who were in the process of buying the *Zaca* invited Flynn and Beverly to a party. It was early evening when Flynn said, "I think I'll lie down. I shall return." In a hallway leading to the hosts' bedroom, Flynn collapsed from a massive heart attack. The fifty-year-old actor was dead on arrival at the hospital. A coroner's report stated that Flynn had died as a result of coronary thrombosis complicated by hardening of the arteries, degeneration of the liver, and an infection of the lower intestine. Errol Flynn's body was that of a very old man.

The corpse was shipped back to California on a freight train. Just before the funeral, a well-known film director and close friend of Flynn sneaked a dozen bottles of whiskey into the star's coffin. Friends agreed that he would have appreciated that gesture. However, he would not have been happy to know that most of the people with whom he had worked in films found excuses not to attend his funeral.

A marker was never placed over Errol Flynn's grave.

Beverly Aadland never became a movie star as Flynn had promised her. A short time after Flynn's death, a man was found shot to death in her bedroom. The coroner ruled it a suicide.

Flynn's parents, both residing in England at the time of his death, died shortly thereafter—his father as a result of a stroke, his mother in a car accident.

Sean, Flynn's only son, became a well-known news photographer. Young Flynn acted in real life the role that his father had played in movies. He went to Vietnam as a correspondent and vanished while covering an assignment during a jungle battle. He was listed as missing and presumed dead.

The *Zaca* was sold, and the new owner sailed it to Europe. During the passage, Errol Flynn's personal flag —a symbolic question mark against a plain background —flew from the mast. Before the return cruise began, the *Zaca,* almost as if in a gesture of defiance, broke down as Flynn's flag waved in the wind high above the decks. It was towed to a shipyard at the French Riviera, where it lay rotting away for years.

But those years of disintegration were not years of inactivity. A number of witnesses reported seeing the eerie specter of Flynn pacing the decks of the vessel. Most often the actor's apparition was seen during the period between sunset and dark. One watchman saw the ghost, jumped overboard, and was in a state of shock when pulled from the water.

A skipper of the vessel moored near the late actor's yacht also witnessed some strange goings-on aboard the *Zaca.* "One night there was music coming from the *Zaca.* You could hear girls' voices and laughter, and the lights on board were going off and on," he said. "It was as though a wild party was going on. But there couldn't have been a party, because no one was aboard. There wasn't even any electricity on her. Something strange was going on."

Could it be that the disturbed spirit of Errol Flynn seeks in death the happiness that he was never able to find in life?

The owners of the shipyard where the rotting hulk of the *Black Witch,* as the *Zaca* is sometimes called, lies recently decided to restore the 118-foot vessel. But there was a problem—Flynn's ghost.

Thus, it was decided to hold an exorcism to banish Flynn's ghost. A thirty-inch-long model of the *Zaca* to be used for the exorcism was taken to a Monte Carlo church on December 18, 1978, by a boat painter who had seen the apparition while working on the yacht. Others who had seen the ghost were also present. Conducting the service were an Anglican archdeacon and a Catholic priest.

As the ritual began, the archdeacon removed salt from a glass container and uttered, "I exorcise thee, O creature of salt, by our living God. Let the spirit of pestilence abide here no more, nor the breath of moral perversion. Let every unclean spirit fly hence." As the archdeacon's chant echoed through the incense-laden air of the church, the boat painter let out a low moan and slumped forward in his pew as though he were possessed. Within a few minutes he seemed all right again.

The archdeacon went on, "Send thy holy angels from Heaven above to protect and cherish all those who go aboard this ship. Let the *Zaca* be hallowed. Let cheer, joy, and health be given to all aboard *Zaca*. Deliver this vessel and all who board her from evil." The ritual took twenty minutes.

Afterward, the priest said, "I am positive that the spirits of evil have departed, and the peace of God shall be with the boat. I prayed from my heart for Errol Flynn, for I remember his face. I hope that he may enter the Kingdom of God, where he may find eternal peace."

Everyone who participated in the ceremony felt that it was a success. But they didn't take into account that it had been held in a church rather than aboard the *Zaca,* and Errol Flynn would never have been caught dead in a church.

How can one be sure that Flynn's ghost no longer roams the deck of the *Zaca?* Very simply—just spend a night aboard it—alone.

Aside from being movie stars, John Wayne and Errol Flynn had little in common. Wayne was greatly admired and respected by his peers. He was a hero. Flynn was a self-admitted rogue. However, both men loved the sea. While the *Zaca* was but one of a score of Flynn's mistresses, the *Wild Goose* was John Wayne's only mistress.

Just a few weeks before his death, John Wayne sold the *Wild Goose* to a Santa Monica attorney.

Some people who've been aboard the *Wild Goose* since

the superstar's demise have felt his presence. A reporter wrote, "John Wayne is dead. But his 'True Grit' spirit still walks the decks of his beloved yacht, the *Wild Goose*."

"I feel he [Wayne] is on board everywhere I look," said the new owner. "Sometimes when I'm in his stateroom, sleeping in his bed, I wake up at two or three in the morning knowing that his presence is there."

I asked the new owner if he'd ever had any experience other than just a feeling of presence. He replied, "A guest who was spending the night aboard the *Wild Goose* got up about three in the morning and noticed the shadowy figure of a man standing in the darkness about ten feet away. Thinking it was me standing there, my guest addressed the figure. The figure's response was to back off into the darkness and vanish. My guest rushed to the porthole of the master stateroom and looked in at me. I was sound asleep in John Wayne's custom-built king-sized bed. There was no way I could have made it into the stateroom before my guest reached the porthole. There was no one else aboard at the time."

Later, when the guest described the incident, the owner asked what the stranger looked like. The apparition was too tall to have been the owner, a member of the crew, or anyone else who could possibly have come aboard that night. The figure seemed to be about six feet four inches tall and to weigh about 225 pounds—very close to the "Duke's" physique.

When I mentioned the recent exorcism rites aboard Errol Flynn's yacht, the new owner said, "Never on this ship. As far as I'm concerned, it's a friendly spirit that we have here. And if indeed it is John Wayne, he's welcome aboard."

The owner went on to tell me about a strange incident concerning some of the lamps aboard the ship. "I went to a place that sold used nautical equipment and bought some brass hurricane lamps that I thought were quite rare and unusual-looking and would look good on the galley bulkhead. After they were put up, the ship's engineer walked into the galley, saw the lanterns, and said, 'I took those lights down years ago and stashed 'em away below. John Wayne had me take them down because he was always bumping his head on them.' The engineer was even more surprised when I told him that I had bought the lamps. We went below where the original lamps had been stowed. They were there, and they were identical to the ones I'd bought. These are very unusual-looking lights, and the chances of finding matching ones would be something like one in ten thousand.

"I left the hurricane lamps hanging in the galley. That night I had difficulty falling asleep. When I finally did doze off, it wasn't for long. I woke up about three in the morning, and the presence of John Wayne in the master stateroom was very strong. Never before had I felt his presence that much. John Wayne was there—I know it. I got up to walk around, and it was as if he was following me wherever I went."

John Wayne was one of the few Hollywood celebrities who could run his own yacht. He had grown up around boats. Although he had done a lot of sailing, he still considered himself a power-boat man. He was as good a seaman off the screen as he was a cowboy or cavalryman on the screen. During a North Atlantic crossing, the *Wild Goose* encountered a violent gale. The vessel was rolling as much as forty-five degrees. The crew, most of them seasick, were huddled below decks, praying. Wayne managed to get about half of them topside. But some of them, thinking the *Wild Goose* would sink, went back below. With almost no assistance, the "Duke" guided his ship safely through the storm.

John Wayne was a believer in life after death. He didn't think that dying was the end of life. His favorite drinking toast was "May you live forever ... and the last voice you hear be mine."

After Wayne's death, his estranged wife said, "I would have done anything, even given my life, to bring him back." Maybe John Wayne—superstar, super patriot, and super sailor—is back ... aboard the *Wild Goose*.

No doubt there are other known ghosts or entities pacing the decks of ships. Some spirits have even been known to follow ships, such as in the case of the Cities Service oil tanker *Watertown*. The spirits were those of two deckhands, James T. Courtney and Michael Meehan, who were asphyxiated while cleaning an empty cargo tank on December 2, 1929. Two days later, the captain consigned the victims' bodies to the deep shortly before sunset. The vessel, en route from San Pedro, California, to New Orleans, via the Panama Canal, was steaming off the coast of Mexico a few days out of California at the time.

The day after the burial at sea, a number of crewmen sighted apparitions of Courtney and Meehan swimming alongside the *Watertown*. The ghosts remained with the ship for several days—even changing course with the vessel. When the ship neared Balboa, at the west end of the canal, the ghosts vanished.

The captain reported the incident upon arrival at New Orleans. For the return trip back to California, company officials provided him with a camera with which to photograph the apparitions.

As soon as the *Watertown* cleared the Panama Canal and steamed out into the Pacific, Courtney and Meehan reappeared. Pictures were taken of the pair, and, upon arrival in San Pedro, company officials had the film developed. It was an eight-exposure roll. None of the first seven pictures came out. The eighth showed the manifestations of the two dead crewmen in the water alongside the moving ship. Experts checked the negative and the print and found both to be authentic. For years an enlargement of the picture of the swimming ghosts hung in Cities Service's New York office.

Joshua Slocum was the first man to sail alone around the world in a small boat. He performed the circumnavigation seventy years before Sir Francis Chichester achieved fame and glory for the same feat.

At one point during Slocum's three-year voyage, which began in 1895, he was off the Azore Islands in the mid-Atlantic when he became violently ill and dragged himself below in the *Spray*, as he had named the thirty-eight-foot yawl. As he lay doubled up in pain on the floor of the cabin, a storm struck. But the fifty-year old Slocum was too sick to return topside and shorten the sails. He lost consciousness.

Some hours later he awakened. The gale was still

howling. Looking out the companionway, Slocum saw, to his astonishment, a man at the helm, holding the *Spray* on a steady course in spite of the wild seas. The mysterious helmsman was dressed in clothing of centuries past. The stranger introduced himself as being a member of Columbus' crew, the pilot of the *Pinta*. He said that he had come to guide Slocum's ship that night.

When Slocum awoke the next morning, he had recovered enough to go on deck. The gale had moderated and the sun was shining. The strange helmsman was nowhere to be seen. Everything on deck that had not been secured had washed away during the night. Salt spray had whitened the decks. The gale had been more severe than Slocum had imagined. Yet, the sails that he had been too sick to furl were still set and pulling. They should have been ripped to shreds. Then Slocum discovered that the *Spray* had gone ninety miles, right on course, during the night. Only an expert helmsman could have made that possible—even if it was a phantom pilot.

Down through the years there have been other reports of crews of ghosts saving both vessels and lives. One of the most recent involved Bob Fowler, a Florida sailor who attempted a single-handed trans-Atlantic voyage in an eighteen-foot sailboat, the *Miskeeter,* during the summer of 1978.

Bob spends most of his spare time working on his plan to be the first American to sail alone nonstop around the world in 1980 or '81. The boat has been designed, the route has been charted, and now a sponsor is being sought. Why does Bob, whose business takes him all around the world by jets flying at five or six hundred miles per hour, seek to travel on his own by one of the slowest and oldest modes of nautical conveyance—especially after his experience in the North Atlantic aboard the *Miskeeter?*

Bob Fowler put to sea from Palm Beach on June 10, 1978. It was a bright, sunny day with only a few scattered clouds. The sea was fairly calm. But the fine sailing weather was not to last. During the first night, while off Ft. Pierce, Florida, a squall bore down on the eighteen-foot sloop. "From then on," said Bob, "it was bad weather all the way. You might say I sailed from bad weather to worse weather.

"I was sailing the great circle route, and when I reached forty-four degrees north, WWV radio began warning of bad weather on the two northernmost Atlantic shipping routes. I made an effort to get as far south as possible, but since *Miskeeter* has no auxiliary engine, I had made it only to about forty degrees north when the first of the really bad fronts caught me."

Winds and seas were quickly up to force nine and gusts were as high as sixty knots. From then on, the voyage was a nightmare for Fowler. The fifteen- to twenty-foot seas looked fifty feet high from the cockpit of the eighteen-foot sailboat. All sails except a twenty-four-square-foot spitfire had been taken in. But still *Miskeeter* seemed to be under water as much as above it. Each breaking wave gave a hissing sound that ended with a reverberating boom against the boat. The wind screamed through the rigging. At times, the tiny vessel overrode a wave crest, and, for what seemed an eternity, the bottom of the world would fall out until a sudden crashing impact brought back the harsh reality of an environment gone mad.

Large ships that couldn't get far enough south to be out of the storm's path were having a rough time, too. But for Bob Fowler it was hell. He couldn't carry out necessary body functions, couldn't eat, and was unable even to reach for a sip of water, for he was hanging on for dear life. Never had he imagined that the sea could be so unpredictable.

No sleep, no food, no water—nothing but barely hanging on to life for four days. "I lay strapped in my bunk, in a state of constant apprehension, almost waiting to die as the seas crashed over my boat. I had done everything possible to secure the boat, and I had been awake for ninety hours. Exhaustion had obviously taken its toll, for then I saw them—three sailors, all wearing tan shirts and pants like a modern yachting crew. They were even wearing nonskid boat shoes. The sailors looked like anyone you'd see at a marina. I was so taken aback that I became oblivious to the aches and pains from all the bruises on my body, caused from being slammed about. Because of my state of fatigue, I knew I had to be hallucinating. I knew it had to be my imagination. I'm not a believer in the supernatural. It's very easy to see something that isn't there when you're exhausted and hungry.

"Besides, I don't know how four of us could get into that little cabin. I just don't think it was anything other than my imagination. Other lone-sailors have had the same experience when things got precarious at sea. They've all been through it. I've talked to a number of them. Really, there's nothing supernatural or strange about it."

Fowler was quite sincere in his skepticism. Maybe his ordeal *had* caused his mind to play tricks on him. And, then again, maybe not.

"Then," said Fowler, "they began discussing among themselves the best storm tactics. Should we lay a hull, should we run with or without warps. 'Don't run,' one of them advised. 'Her length is too short and she'll pitchpole.' 'Lay a hull and hold on,' another suggested. It seemed so real and clear. I couldn't recognize any of their faces. One of them said, 'We can't let him take the helm—he's too sleepy; and if he runs off before the wind, he'll kill us all.'

"They were mocking me and calling me a poor sailor," Fowler continued. "One of them said, 'Push him, he's going to fall asleep. Don't let him sleep.' It was just like having a nightmare, and you're trying to wake up but can't. Then one of the sailors said, 'Next time we sign on as crew, we'll make sure we don't get a sleepy-head.' "

Although Bob kept reiterating his doubts as to the reality of his phantom crew, I got the feeling that deep down he hadn't totally convinced himself. The further his story progressed, the more intrigued I became.

"They kept mocking my seamanship. 'You didn't lash the tiller tight enough. It's come loose. Get up there and secure it before you lose the rudder. Go on, get topside and check it.' Holding on to anything I could get a grip on, I dragged myself on deck, and to my amazement, the tiller had come unlashed and was slapping from side to side. I relashed it, struggled back below, and collapsed in my bunk. But I couldn't sleep, because they kept at me. I begged and pleaded with them to leave me alone, but they kept on talking for what seemed like hours. 'Go check your battery. The cap's come off and the acid is leaking,' said one of them, who was wearing a blue windbreaker. But I was too weak to move. And still they kept at me. I don't know which was worse, them or the storm.

"Hour after hour they nagged at me. Finally they convinced me that I'd never reach my destination, which was Plymouth, England. Then, to my astonishment, one of them said, 'Take your flare gun and go on deck. There's a ship out there.'

"With what seemed like the last of my strength, I managed to crawl out on deck with my flare gun. I couldn't believe what I saw—a ship in the distance. I fired off six flares in rapid succession.

"Within minutes the ship, the Finnish freighter *M/V Andrew,* bound for Baltimore with a cargo of newsprint, was alongside. But the seas were too rough for them to take me and the *Miskeeter* aboard. The ship lay to, waiting for the seas to subside. I went back below and found that the three sailors who had been tormenting me were gone."

Some hours later, Fowler and the *Miskeeter* were aboard the *Andrew,* en route to Baltimore.

When I interviewed Fowler at his office more than a years after his strange voyage, he was still convinced his spectral shipmates were but figments of his imagination. Yet, how does one account for the fact that the phantom sailors warned him about the tiller coming unlashed, told him that he'd never reach his destination, and alerted him to the presence of a passing ship?

One more thing: after being taken aboard the *Andrew,* Fowler slept for twelve hours. After awakening and taking some food, his first in more than four days, he examined the *Miskeeter,* which had been hoisted board the freighter's deck and lashed down. When he opened the cockpit locker, he saw that one of the caps was missing from the battery and acid had been leaking out of it. Although the locker had not been open during the storm, the missing battery cap was nowhere to be found.

Hallucinations, figments of the imagination, phantom

sailors, or whatever the ghostly mariners were, the fact remains that they may have saved Robert Fowler and his little ship.

Not all occurences involving maritime ghosts happen on the high seas or in harbors bordering those oceans. Incidents relating to nautical manifestations have taken place hundreds of miles inland. There is a stretch of the Mississippi River in the areas of Natchez, Vicksburg, and St. Joseph where strange things have happened, and still are happening. The region abounds with Indian lore of spirits and the supernatural.

At certain times, weird screams are heard coming from the middle of the river. The cries sound like the voice of a woman. They are followed by the French words, *"Gaston! Gaston! Aidez-moi au nom de Dieu! Les hommes me blessent!"* (Gaston! Help me in the name of God! The men are hurting me!) People living in the area who've heard the screams believe that they have something to do with the river steamer, *Iron Mountain*, and its unknown fate more than a hundred years ago.

The *Iron Mountain* was a large Mississippi paddle-wheel steamer that plied the Mississippi and Ohio Rivers between New Orleans and Pittsburgh during the post–Civil War era. The vessels were like floating towns with their own theatrical groups, gamblers, musicians, prostitutes and various other diversions.

The *Iron Mountain* was in excess of one hundred and eighty feet in length, and she had a beam of thirty-five feet. In addition to carrying passengers, she towed freight barges. The vessel's calliope could be heard long before the smoke from her belching stacks could be seen as she approached her various towns of call. And wherever she called, a holiday atmosphere reigned.

In June, 1874, the *Iron Mountain* cast off from her wharf at Vicksburg and set out for New Orleans. She was carrying fifty-seven passengers and towing a string of barges. As she reached mid-stream and approached a bend, her pilot gave a long blast on the steamboat's whistle. The *Iron Mountain* rounded the bend and was never seen aagin.

The barges were found with the tow ropes cut clean

through. No trace of wreckage from the big steamer or dead bodies were ever found. The paddle steamer, *Iron Mountain,* had simply vanished. Hundreds of miles of river bottom were dragged but without success.

Other riverboats steaming upstream should have passed the *Iron Mountain.* None reported seeing her. Except for a few deep holes that were thoroughly dragged, there was no water sufficiently deep to completely cover the huge vessel. Had she been wrecked or burned, there would have been bodies and debris. There seems to be no earthly explanation for the disappearance of the *Iron Mountain.*

Although not one shred of evidence revealing the fate of the big riverboat or its passengers was ever found, local people feel that the spirit of one of its passenger is still around and might someday give a clue, via a spiritualist medium, as to what happened just south of Vicksburg.

Many theories have been formulated, but only one seems to be more than conjecture. Because river pirates prowled the waters of the Mississippi in the years following the Civil War, local people think that the *Iron Mountain* was captured by these pirates, who, after an orgy of rape and killing, buried the bodies, dismantled the steamer and secreted the sections where they would never be found. Records show that there were several French-speaking passengers aboard the steamer.

Eleven months after the *Iron Mountain* disappeared forever, another palatial Mississippi River paddlewheel boat, the *Mississippi Queen* cast off from Memphis on April 17, 1873. Like the ill-fated *Iron Mountain,* her destination was New Orleans. She was last seen shortly before midnight, about twelve hours after her departure. Then she, too, vanished without a trace down the Mississippi.

It is often stated that an apparition or ghost derives from a combination of the energy from the deceased's body and his psyche, spirit, intelligence or soul. If that is true, then it makes it even more astounding for an inanimate object to return as a ghost. But it does happen, as is the case of the spectral square-rigged sailing ship that plies on to her fiery doom almost every year either immediately before or right after the sun's autumnal equinox over Nova Scotia.

Merigomash is a small fishing village located on Nova Scotia's north shore, south of Prince Edward Island near where the eastern part of the Northumberland Strait joins the Gulf of the St. Lawrence. It is just off-shore from Merigomash where the phantom vessel is seen. In the early part of December, 1953, according to Associated Press, hundreds of people observed the specter ship making almost nightly manifestations.

As each autumn turns into winter, shore dwellers keep a regular vigil for the strange specter. When it appears, phones ring and roads become jammed with folks rushing down to the wooded shore to witness the unbelievable.

As the ship moves into view on a northeasterly course, with every rag of canvas her three masts can carry, a deathlike silence reigns over the crowds of spectators who can't believe what they are seeing. But why does she move so fast—even when there is no wind blowing? And if there is a fog or haze, her outline glows as though phosphorescent. Those running along the shore on foot or horseback cannot keep up with her.

Soon ominous lights appear to be moving along her sloping decks. Then, suddenly, the phantom vessel shudders as though she has run aground. Shadowy figures are racing along her length. But before any of them reach where they are running to, the vessel is engulfed in flames. Burning topmasts and yardarms crash to the deck. Obscure figures begin jumping over the side. Then, as the spectral ship is completely engulfed in flames from stem to stern, she plunges bow first down into the dark water—and the night is black once again.

The ghost ship with its phantom crew has been intriguing Nova Scotians for well over a hundred years. Although the identity of the vessel is unknown, most natives of the area attribute it to a pirate ship that in years gone by went down with all hands in those straits.

Is there really a ghost ship that plies the waters south of Prince Edward Island each December? Or could it be that hundreds of God-fearing people are merely hallucinating. Then, maybe, it is a time warp that has never been able to escape the confines of earth. Another possibility could be that the deeds of the pirate crew were so blasphemous, that they've been condemned to relive their own deaths on each anniversary. Who knows?

> *Headaches and heartaches and all kinds of pain*
> *Are not apart from a railroad train;*
> *Tales that are earnest, noble and gran'*
> *Belong to the life of a railroad man.*
>
> Anonymous
> ("Casey Jones")

8

Ghosts of the Railroad

There were days when men, not computers, ran the nation's trains. Railroadmen were folk heroes back then. What little boy didn't want to be a railroad engineer when he grew up? Until the advent of the diesel locomotive, there were probably more legends about trainmen than men of any other profession. An engineer's skill was judged not only by how well he could handle his locomotive but by how many notes he could play on his steam whistle.

Almost everyone has heard of Casey Jones, but few have heard of Joe Baldwin. He was a conductor for the Wilmington, Manchester, and Augusta Railway, which later became part of the Atlantic Coast Line. The railroad ran through most of Georgia and the Carolinas.

On a moist, warm spring evening in 1889, a train carrying Grover Cleveland halted for fuel and water at a whistle-stop called Maco Station, about twelve miles west of Wilmington, North Carolina. During the stop, President Cleveland got off the train and took a stroll along the right-of-way. Looking down the tracks, he saw a signalman carrying a red and a green lantern. He asked the conductor why two colored lanterns were being used instead of the usual single white one. The conductor replied, "Well, sir, you may think it strange, but if the signalman didn't carry red and green lights, there'd be no way for the engineers on trains coming down the line to know whether or not it was the ghost of Joe Baldwin looking for its head."

The conductor then went on to tell Joe Baldwin's story. "For a fact, Mr. President, it was back in 1868 on a damp spring night just like this. It had been raining all day but it let up about dark. A freight train was coming down these tracks about a mile up the line, heading for the siding at Maco so it could let an express train pass. Well, Joe Baldwin was the conductor riding alone in the caboose. Suddenly he felt the 'crummy'—that's what we call the caboose—slowing down. Looking out the window, he discovered that the car he was in had come uncoupled from the rest of the train.

"Hearing the whistle of the oncoming express, Joe Baldwin grabbed his lantern and started for the rear platform. Then he saw it—the headlight of the express coming down the tracks. He was standing on the rear platform of the caboose, frantically waving his lantern, when the express engine hit. There was an explosion of iron and wood.

"The next morning searchers found Joe's lantern over there in that swamp. Then they found his mangled body in the smashed caboose way down the tracks. His head had been torn clean off his body. They never did find Joe Baldwin's head.

"It's been more than twenty-two years now since the accident, but still, every once in a while a train crew will see a lantern moving along the tracks. But it's just the lantern moving—nobody's carrying it. So, Mr. President, what else can it be except Joe Baldwin looking for his missing head?"

President Cleveland nodded and climbed back aboard his private car.

Now, almost 125 years after Joe Baldwin's death, the spectral lantern is still seen sometimes along the tracks west of Wilmington near the edge of the swamp.

Skeptics who have seen the light attribute it not to Joe

Baldwin's ghost but to lights from automobiles on highway 87 a quarter of a mile away. They say that under certain atmospheric conditions, the automobiles' headlights flicker along the tracks and appear to be a lantern moving down the right-of-way. This is correct. When conditions are just right, there is that effect—a light, way down the tracks, only a slight flicker at first, like a firefly. Then it starts moving alongside the rails and keeps increasing in size until it gets close enough to resemble a lantern with its yellow oil-fueled flame. But how does one account for that phenomenon back in the days before the automobile? In fact, a few years ago, state officials closed highway 87 to all traffic for several days. People waited and watched—and they saw Joe Baldwin's lantern moving along the tracks.

Although Maco is not shown on most maps and has fewer than twenty-five families, people come from all over the United States to park at night alongside the tracks, hoping to see Joe Baldwin's lantern, and not many are disappointed.

A United States Army investigation team from nearby Fort Bragg was sent to Maco to investigate the spectral light. They were unable to come up with a solution. Several of the men fired their weapons at the apparition, but to no avail. The light began bouncing around so much that all the shots missed.

Joe Baldwin's ghost still materializes on dark, damp nights as he goes on searching for his severed head. And a hundred years from now, people interested in the occult will still tell of the ghost of Joe Baldwin and his bizarre lantern.

At the edge of every railroad yard, usually close to the roundhouse* or engine yard, it was common to see a sparkling-clean tavern surrounded by soot-covered red-brick buildings. These were the favorite watering holes of the train crews—especially on payday. Some even had rooms upstairs for out-of-town crews laying over for the night. To railroaders, after breathing soot all day on a

---

*A roundhouse is a circular building used for the storage and repair of locomotives.

long freight haul, the drinking establishment at the edge of the railroad yard was like an oasis in the middle of the desert.

In the mid-1950's, steam locomotives were being rapidly phased out by most railroads. Engine crews were being trained, or retrained, to run diesel locomotives. Although diesels were more efficient, they lacked the romance and glory of the steam locomotive.

In January 1955, the Baltimore and Ohio Railroad was in the process of phasing out the last of its steam locomotives. Some were transferred to smaller railroads that operated near the coal fields, a number were exported, a few went to railroad museums, but most were scrapped.

On the night of January 17, 1955, a group of nostalgic, bleary-eyed engineers and firemen were gathered in a bar next to the railroad yards just outside of Toledo, Ohio, sadly toasting the demise of the steam locomotive and recalling their railroad adventures of years gone by. As the evening wore on and the men became even drunker, the talk turned to an old switch engine that had been operating out of the switch yard across the street. The six-wheel locomotive had hauled its last train that day and was to be taken to the scrap yard the following morning.

"Hey, let's take the old girl for one last ride," shouted one of the drinkers.

"No!" cried another. "We'd have to coal and water her and fire up the boiler."

"I was looking at it this afternoon—she's got plenty of coal and water."

"What happens if we get caught?"

"We won't get caught," shouted a tall, burly Virginian. "We'll just stay in the yard, not on the main line."

A number of miles away, a diesel-powered freight train was heading for Toledo. It was due there about 12:30 A.M. The engineer turned to the fireman and said, "It's cold nights like this that make me miss the comfort of a steam-engine cab."

The men from the tavern already had a head of steam on the old switch engine. Passing a bottle around, they gently eased the locomotive ahead. The soot-blackened engine moved silently, if not majestically, down the tracks . . . almost like a black shadow. Souvenir hunters had already removed the bell, whistle, and headlights.

The diesel locomotive, its headlights glaring through the cold night, was now nearing the Baltimore and Ohio freight yards.

Running across the Toledo B & O tracks just outside the yards was a Pennsylvania Railroad (now part of Penn-Central) main line. The B & O freight train was cleared to go on into the yard, as there was no "Pennsy" train due till morning.

The blacked-out switch engine steamed aimlessly around the yards. "Ya know," said the skilled but very drunk man who was taking his turn as engineer, "those damned diesels may be more efficient, but they'll never make a diesel as fast as one of these steamers. Let's see how fast she'll go."

"Wait a minute!" shouted one of his comrades. "Let's get over on that Pennsy main line where we can really open her up. There's nothin' due on those tracks till morning."

They maneuvered the engine through a maze of switches and twisting tracks until it was on the Pennsylvania Railroad's main line.

The diesel freight train was moving along at forty miles per hour. The engineer reached for the throttle, reducing its speed to twenty-five miles per hour as it neared the yards.

The big Virginian, taking his turn for a last fling at running a steam locomotive, slid onto the engineer's seat on the right-hand side of the cab. Shouting, "Let's see what she'll do!" he reached over and moved the "Johnson bar" to full. Black smoke, invisible in the darkness of the night, belched from the stack. Sparks flew as steel wheels ground against steel rails in rhythm with chugging pistons. Slowly the switch engine picked up speed as a device on the locomotive dropped sand onto the rails, giving traction to the spinning drive wheels.

As the long freight train approached the yard, passing a trackside sign with only the letter *W* on it, the engineer reached up and gave a blast of the horn. "Well, we'll be home soon as we cross over the Pennsy tracks ahead."

The old switch engine was racing down the Pennsylvania's tracks at seventy-five miles per hour. "Hell, we can get another thirty out of her!" yelled the engineer. His cronies cheered with approval.

The fireman in the cab of the diesel leaned forward, squinting his eyes. "What's that ahead? Looks like a light on the tracks."

"It is a light," shouted the engineer. "It's a switchman's lantern! He's signaling us to stop." The screeching, brake-locked wheels of the diesel gave a fireworks display as they slid along the tracks.

The men in the cab of the steam engine were oblivious to anything except how fast "their" locomotive was going.

"There's never been a switchman around here before," said the engineer of the diesel as his train ground to a halt only a dozen feet from the Pennsylvania tracks. He and his fireman climbed down from the cab and walked back to where the switchman, who was wearing a plaid macki-naw and a stocking cap, was standing. He was holding the lantern low at his side, so they were unable to see his face. Because of the switch engine's speed, the warning semaphore signal hadn't turned red until the diesel was nearly stopped. As they approached the switchman, they didn't notice that there was no vapor from his breath as he exhaled into the frigid night air. In fact, they didn't notice anything unusual about him at all. Then suddenly the blacked-out steam switch engine with its drunken crew roared out of the darkness just a few feet away on the Pennsylvania tracks. As it raced off into the night, the crew of the diesel turned back toward the switchman. But no one was there. They looked under the train, but there was no place he could have hidden in the few seconds that it took the switch engine to pass. The phantom switchman who had averted a disastrous train wreck had vanished.

The crew of the switch engine never knew, until a reunion years later, how close to death they had come in the early hours of the morning of January 18, 1955.

There have been no other reports of the phantom switchman at Toledo's Baltimore and Ohio Railroad yards. Nor have there been any near-disasters that might have given him reason to be seen. But that doesn't mean he's not around.

If when the wind blows Rattling the trees,
Clicking like skeletons' elbows and knees,
Hoofs of three horses Going abreast—
Turn about, turn about, A closed door is best!
                              Elizabeth J. Coatsworth
                              (*Daniel Webster's Horses*)

9

Animals That Return

It was long believed that only humans could become
ghosts. But if inanimate objects such as cars, ships, air-
planes, and trains can qualify as haunters, what about the
creatures of the animal kingdom?

The late Joy Adamson, the scientist and wildlife re-
searcher who wrote the bestseller *Born Free,* was convinced that animals have telepathic powers. Her research
with a wild-born lioness named Elsa prompted Mrs.
Adamson to say, "Elsa could control her cubs from a
distance of 180 miles." She continued, "Elsa always knew
when George, my husband, and I were coming to see
her. . . . I was intuitively aware of Elsa's death at the
moment it occurred."

How could Elsa, supposedly a reasonless, soulless animal, communicate with Mrs. Adamson at the moment of
her death? Some say it is the love between man and beast
that bridges the gap between life and death. Yet, love is a
human emotion, and experts say that animals are not
capable of experiencing love. However, the serious investigator into animal phenomena will quickly discover that
while Mrs. Adamson's observations of animal communi-

cation were unusual, they were not singularly unique. Animals have been known to solve complex mathematical problems; a psychic horse named Lady not only could see past, present, and future, but could communicate with the human world; Strongheart, a German shepherd of movie fame, performed such incredible feats of ESP that he became the subject of J. Allen Boone's book *Kinship With All Life.*

Is it possible that animals, like man, have souls and survive the death experience to populate other dimensions? Is it possible that animals return in spirit to this world to visit mortals—or to haunt them?

Apparently, such was the case involving two ranch hands who sat playing poker around an old wooden table in a Monterey, Mexico, bunkhouse. A strong-smelling concoction of homemade tequila rested on a nearby sideboard. The stench of liquor, tobacco, and sweat filled the air. Chico patted his massive belly, wiped his greasy mustache with the back of his hand, and belched. "Dammit, Ramon, you can't play cards and you don't shoot straight. You ain't much of a man, are you?"

Chico leaned forward, put down four aces, and, laughing crudely, reached for the pile of money in the middle of the table. However, before he could take the winnings, Ramon lunged forward and grabbed Chico's wrist. "I'm tired of your filthy insults!" he snarled. "Put your money where your mouth is, man—all or nothing at all. You think you're so good with a gun? Well, let's try it with a moving target—double or nothing."

The men rose simultaneously and headed for the bunkhouse door, grabbing the jug of tequila on the way out. The evening sun bathed the scene in an eerie, blood-red glow. The ranch was curiously quiet as the two men searched for a satisfactory target. Suddenly, a small bundle of red-feathered fury streaked out of nowhere. Wings flapped and long, spurred claws ripped at Chico's flesh as he struggled to keep Señor Carlos' prize fighting rooster away from his eyes. When Ramon beat the game cock away from Chico's bloodied head, the bird backed off, protesting vociferously with ruffled feathers and hostile lunges. "You son of a bitch!" screamed Chico, as he reached for his sidearm. "That's the last time you attack me or anyone else!"

Chico wiped the blood from his eyes, pulled back the hammer of his revolver, and with both hands took aim at the strutting rooster. But before he could pull the trigger, Ramon intervened. "Don't shoot yet!" he cried. "Let's take aim from behind that fence over there. We'll each have one shot. Whoever shoots the rooster's head off wins the poker stakes. Okay?"

The two flipped a coin to see who would fire the first shot. Then, after a big gulp from the jug of homemade liquor, they took their places behind a split-rail fence. The prize cock arched its neck defiantly and flapped its bright plumage.

Ramon took the first shot. Reeling drunkenly, he steadied his hand on the fence, pulled back the hammer, and squeezed the trigger. The six-shooter belched fire with a resounding bang that shattered the still evening. Chico roared in delight as Ramon's shot went wild. The stunned rooster barely had time to move before Chico's shot followed. The proud head of the fighting cock exploded off its neck. Chico slapped Ramon on the back and giggled in triumph.

But Chico's drunken victory was not to last. As the men watched in horror, the headless rooster, whose neck had become a spurting fountain of crimson, staggered upright, gaining strength with every passing second. They stared in utter disbelief as the undead creature flew at them in vengeful rage. Chico took the brunt of the attack as his cowardly *compadre* ran back into the bunkhouse. "Help me! I can't see!" screamed Chico. "It's tearing my eyes out!"

Ramon peered warily through the bunkhouse window in a drunken haze, wiping blood and perspiration from the deep gashes inflicted by the decapitated fowl. He stared in disbelief as Chico ran, bellowing in fear and pain, into the gathering darkness, with the headless avenger in close pursuit. Chico was never seen again.

But the headless rooster returned—many times. And the sightings always presaged an awesome, unexpected disaster. Laying hens stopped producing eggs; the señor's prized cattle became infected with deadly anthrax virus; the ranch house was nearly destroyed by a fire of unknown origin. Before each catastrophe, the ghost of the outraged, headless rooster was seen by two or more witnesses. The owner decided to sell the ranch after he too saw the horrible specter. "It's an evil omen," he said with a shudder.

The new owner of the ranch fared no better. The headless thing frightened the other animals, and ranch hands left after only a few days' employment. Finally, a Catholic priest performed a ritual exorcism ceremony to rid the ranch once and for all of the incredible ghostly visitations. The following morning, a disturbance was heard in the henhouse. The new owner was the first to reach the scene. He saw the headless rooster strutting around inside the henhouse, creating havoc among the hens. Crossing himself and calling upon the protection of the Almighty, he backed out of the door.

Two ranch hands ran toward the henhouse, pushed their employer aside, and entered. They too witnessed the terrifying sight, and rushed back out. After the men had calmed down, they armed themselves with pitchforks and reentered the henhouse, determined to find and kill the so-called ghost. They pursued it behind the chicken roost. There was no way out. The creature was trapped. One man clutched his pitchfork and waited expectantly as the other crawled under the wooden perch. But it was as if the winged horror had evaporated—and it had, too. For it was not flesh and blood but a ghostly thing.

The owner paid his employees, sold his animals and equipment, then abandoned the ranch forever. No citizen of Monterrey will go near the haunted ranch that is cursed with the spectral presence of a doom-dealing headless rooster.

Nearly every type of animal has at one time or another become a haunter. But the well-documented account of Gref, the talking mongoose, is without doubt the most incredible and unusual case of an animal ghost.

A mongoose is a weasel-like creature, well known as a fearless killer of poisonous snakes. The life and times of Gref, the talking mongoose of Doarl Cashen on the Isle of

Man in Great Britain, has added extensively to our present knowledge and bewilderment regarding the mysterious powers of animals. Gref, the articulate mongoose, lodged himself securely in the walls of a farmhouse owned by the James T. Irving family. His vocalizing was so unique and clamorous that Gref soon became an object for investigation by British researchers and naturalists. By his own definition, Gref claimed to be a "ghost," a spirit from another world. When pressed for answers as to his unusual abilities, he replied, "I'm a freak, a ghost, and part of the fifth dimension."

Gref terrorized the local population for quite some time before he met his demise at the hands of a superstitious human being. But past experience with other animal ghosts might have fostered fear in the heart of Gref's killer. The Isle of Man is a small, closely knit English community. Tales are passed from generation to generation and many times are grossly exaggerated in the repetition. But not so in the case of another English animal ghost who might have inspired Gref's execution. Like Señor Carlos' prize rooster, it too lost its head—but returned to haunt.

Manchester, England, with its conservative citizens and stately Tudor mansions, seems hardly the place for the unexplainable presence of an animal ghost. But many have witnessed its unsettling antics.

On a chilly October evening, before the turn of the century, a local clergyman and his brother-in-law sat drinking brandy near the fireplace in a Lower Seedley Road cottage adjacent to an old church. The embers glowed eerily in the darkness of the evening as the flames burned lower and lower. The reverend took an iron poker and stirred the embers to a burst of flame.

"It's getting quite late," said Richard, as he made ready to retire for the evening.

The reverend arose to bid his houseguest good night. As he did so, he tossed his half-spent cigar into the glowing coals on the hearth. Suddenly, the two men stared in disbelief as an image emerged from the fireplace. The lit end of the cigar seemed to take the form of an evil, staring red eye that floated ominously above the mantel. It seemed to glow with menacing hatred as it glared at them from above.

The huge, threatening red eye remained elevated in midair as it floated toward the men. Richard reached for the iron poker and struck repeatedly at the unholy object, but it evaded his efforts to destroy it. The two men were transfixed with horror as the grandfather clock in the foyer struck midnight. Then a rush of unusually frigid air engulfed them, as the semblance of a ghostly, headless cat appeared from nowhere and seemed to chase the evil, glaring eye out of the room and into the foyer.

The two agreed not to tell anyone of that night's scene of terror. After considerable discussion and several more glasses of sherry, they retired for the night to a fitful sleep.

The following evening, the reverend and his wife were awakened by frantic barking. Every dog in the neighborhood had joined in the noisy serenade. Husband and wife rushed downstairs to investigate. The reverend cautiously lifted the door latch, only to be forced back as a rush of incredibly cold air swept past him. The gust was too frigid for an October night, and in its wake followed the body of a fearful-looking decapitated cat, which scampered past them and disappeared into the study.

The reverend's wife's horrified scream echoed through the night, awakening their houseguest, who charged downstairs, brandishing a loaded revolver.

"It was a dreadful headless creature!" shrieked the reverend's wife.

The two men exchanged a knowing glance. For they knew it was the same incredible phantom that had appeared to them out of the study fireplace the preceding night.

The following day, the children of the household burst into the cottage, wide-eyed with excitement. "There's a mean black dog outside! It's gone mad and torn the head off a cat!" they cried. "Come quickly!'

When the adults followed the children into the courtyard, there was no sign of the dog, nor were there any bloodied remains of a decapitated cat. But, as the onlookers stared incredulously, the ghastly headless cat appeared mysteriously before them. It appeared to pursue an invisible enemy out of the courtyard and into the surrounding countryside, kicking up a flurry of dry fall leaves as it skittered out of sight.

The strange visitation was reported to local police. But the clergyman and his family moved out of the haunted house the following day, fleeing the vengeful feline ghost that forever pursues the specter of a mad killer-dog through the long fall nights.

Great Britain, the haunted isle, has no monopoly on frightening animal specters. For generations, numerous accounts of American animal haunters have been reported. The wildly galloping black stallion that haunts the country roads and hollows of rural Columbia, Tennessee, has become a local legend. Since the aftermath of the Civil War, the devil horse of Ghost Hollow has befuddled and occasionally terrified local citizens.

It was springtime in the hill country and new life blossomed everywhere. Yet, death was very near as the hooves of a great black war stallion pounded out a steady rhythm on the hard, red-clay road. Sweat glistened on both horse and rider—but for different reasons. The black stallion thrilled to the smell of blood and the sounds of battle, for he had been bred purposely to lead his master into the din. But the blue-uniformed rider sat uneasily in the saddle, preparing to lead his men into unfamiliar territory. The terrain was heavy with timber, and the hills could easily hide an enemy. For many long years, warrior and charger had ridden undaunted into the thickest of conflagrations. But this time was to be different, as animal and man sensed the impending ambush—too late. With swords drawn, the soldiers defended themselves against the unexpected assault. The first bullet fired by the soldiers in gray ripped deep into the chest of the Yankee cavalryman. Spurting a crimson tide of blood, he fell forward, clutching his magnificent steed's black mane. The fiery-eyed charger, his heart filled with blood-lust, knew only the momentary glory of battle as he raced on into the thick of the fray.

Only too quickly the battle ended. The dying soldier slid slowly from the saddle as the great horse stood trembling with excitement. The noble, sensitive animal turned his head as he caught the scent of an unwelcome death, and began to nuzzle his dead master, bumping him gently as if trying to awaken him. The beast stood by the side of his fallen master throughout that dark night. When the enemy was finally routed and comrades-in-arms attempted to bury the dead soldier, the war stallion struck out, nostrils flared and deadly hooves tearing the air in a misguided effort to protect his master. Thinking the horse had gone mad, an officer shot him through the skull.

But Snow Creek Road still rings with the eerie sound of the charger's shod hooves. It's a narrow road with treacherous, crooked turns that obscure the view. Yet, many have heard the ghost horse's pounding hoofbeats, and, thinking a runaway horse will soon overtake them, they make for the underbrush by the roadside. Then, the phantom stallion gallops past. As witnesses stare in disbelief, the sound rapidly fades into the distance.

Hoofprints are never found, but occasionally the animal is seen. A wild horse in tobacco country is not to be taken lightly, especially in springtime when plant beds are brimming with young shoots. Often, authorities are advised that the phantom horse has been observed tearing up the countryside. However, the horse is never found, and the damaged property appears miraculously restored. But the description of the culprit is always the same.

Once, a farmer called out to the spectral horse, "Whoa, fellow, whoa!" He heard the creature snort and pull up to an abrupt halt, shuffle momentarily, then gallop off in the opposite direction. Yet, nothing was visible to the eye.

Is the restless spirit of the black stallion a ghost, or was the trauma of horse and rider during their last battle so intense that the memory of the event is forever impressed on the local countryside? In the spring of each year, when the hills come alive, a dead creature is reborn from the distant past and comes back to the world of the living— to haunt.

Horror upon horror. Shock upon shock....
The vocabulary of grief and disbelief stretches
only so far.... At the end of a week of in-
credible headlines, all of us were left stunned,
exhausted, overwhelmed by the flood of bloody
"senseless" information.... It was all sense-
less. And, yet, there must be a thread connect-
ing all this violence.

Herb Caen
(*San Francisco Chronicle*)

10

Cult of the Undead

With the coming of dusk in the jungles of Guyana, when nocturnal sounds begin overwhelming the calls of day creatures, strange things begin to occur in the area of Jonestown. New sounds coming from the forsaken commune echo throughout the surrounding rain forest. They are not the cries of jungle creatures, nor are they the din of anything human. Those who've heard them say they are the screams of the undead. The green hell is permeated by a sense of fear. Neither the horrendous howls of the jaguars, nor the ear shattering screech of the blood-thirsty vampire bats stir the emotions as do the awesome voices from the cult of the undead.

One can only guess at how many of the nearly one thousand souls who, at Jim Jones' command, suffered a torturous death still roam the ghastly compound as restless spirits. The Guyanian authorities have closed the area to all outsiders. But who would want to be there, especially after dark?

There are times when all of the customary sounds of the night cease, and an eerie pall of silence reigns over the jungle. For something sinister stalks the huge vine-covered trees and giant clusters of orchids ... something that even jolts fear into the wildlife. It is Jim Jones—or rather his ghost—that still roams the site of the most bizarre commune of modern times.

Jonestown was a place of voluntary slavery. Each day was interspersed with trauma for all but Jim Jones and his closest henchmen. The inhabitants were too busy slaving away in the crop-filled fields to realize what was happening to their lives. Hard work and drugs kept the cultists subservient. Jim Jones, communist, con-man, bi-sexual, and slavemaster, was their leader, high priest, king and god. He had total control of his followers' lives. Adultery committed by anyone but Jones or his immediate assistants was a severely punishable offense. Even husbands and wives had to seek permission from Jones to engage in sexual intercourse with each other. On occasion, married couples who were caught defying their leader's ban against sex without his permission were made to copulate in front of an assemblage of the entire Jonestown communal populace. Yet, his congregation was peppered with his personally sired offspring.

Though he himself preferred the body of a man or a boy to that of a woman, Jones declared homosexual activity, when committed by others, an unpardonable crime with dire consequences for the offenders.

New members gave all income and property to the church and to Jones, who had them believing that he was Jesus Christ reincarnated. Millions of dollars in cash and jewelry were stashed away at the commune headquarters. Most of the monies were intended for transporting Jones and his followers to Russia where they thought they would "find a better life." Negotiations with Soviet diplomats in Guyana were already underway well in advance of the notorious massacre.

Jim Jones was a despicable criminal who demanded that his followers call him "Father" or "Dad" and worship him as God. He was once a Fundamentalist preacher in Indiana. He claimed to be part American Indian in order to be more readily accepted by minority groups, even though he was actually of Welsh descent. He and his wife Marceline, a registered nurse, had spent time in Brazil studying the arts of pseudo psychic trickery and faith healing. He was an advocate of communal socialism, and when he wasn't convincing his followers he was Jesus Christ returned to life, he would tell them he was Lenin, the father of communism, reincarnated. Sometimes he'd place more emphasis on communism and at other times Christianity—whatever served Jim Jones' needs the most was the rule of the day.

There was very little, if any, racial discrimination at Jonestown—or at least not on the surface, for eighty percent of the inhabitants were black. Only those who came from the most humble ghetto life found Jonestown an improvement in their living conditions. Those members of the cult with low emotional drives, no great ambitions in life and a need to belong—to anyone who'd accept them—found life at Jonestown more than just bearable. For the others there was no escape. Many believed in Jones' claims to be able to do anything from placing fatal curses on his enemies to raising the dead. He was an expert at brainwashing. And there were enough contented members of the cult to keep any malcontents from fleeing.

The stage for the impending cataclysm was actually set thousands of miles away from the steaming death-filled jungle of Guyana.

California is the mecca for America's social turncoats. The golden state is a strange state, and few deny it. Both good and evil forces are at work there. And destiny unerringly pointed a blood-stained finger at one particular area of California and marked it for all time as the favorite city of every misfit—"The Kook Capital." From the fogenshrouded shores of the San Francisco Bay area a pall of unparalleled cultist violence has emerged since the turn of the century. In the last two decades alone there were the infamous Charles Manson cult of marauding murderers; the black "Zebra Killers" striking out randomly at white citizens; Patty Hearst and the Symbionese Liberation Army; the self-confessed Zodiac killer and his alleged thirty-seven victims; and the two female cultists, Lynette "Squeaky" Fromme and Sara Jane Moore who both made attempts on President Gerald Ford's life.

The People's Temple, whose operating capital was its members' life savings, social security and pension checks, had its beginnings in the greater San Francisco area. Hun-

dreds of believers joined the cult. Those who had nothing
to begin with or had already given everything they owned
to the People's Temple were usually allowed to defect
without much ado. But when a member who still had a
substantial source of income, even if it was only Social
Security payments, became disillusioned with the sect,
Jones would use a considerable amount of persuasion to
retain their membership. When that failed, the defector
was subject to dire consequences. Some died mysteriously
while others simply vanished.

Tax deductible contributions received by the People's
Temple were meant to enhance the lifestyle of its members. But instead the funds were used to bribe, coerce,
bargain and buy positions of power and political authority
for Jones. But when citizens and honest politicians became
suspicious of what Jones and his People's Temple stood
for and its philosophies, the business end of the cult became less profitable. Jones had serious legal problems, too,
and had been advised to move his flock away from the
growing hostility of northern California and possible ar-
rest. He and his devotees began relocating the cult members to Guyana where an agricultural commune was established to protect the Temple from constant public scrutiny.
Few of the cultists were aware of the difficulties to come.
The first to arrive were not allowed to communicate with
their brethren still in California about the rigors and
misery they were forced to endure. All mail was censored,
and only Jones' most trusted disciples were permitted to
travel to Georgetown, the capital of Guyana.

In spite of Jones' security measures, word did get back
to California—word not only of hardships but also of
some members being restrained from leaving Jonestown.
When California Congressman Leo J. Ryan heard of what
was going on, he began an immediate investigation, the result of which incited him to personally visit Guyana and
Jonestown.

When news of Rep. Ryan's impending trip to South
America was released, a number of news reporters asked
and were allowed to accompany him. One, Bob Brown, a
TV newsreel cameraman, began acting strangely when his
employer gave him the assignment. He discussed terms of
his will and insurance policies with his family. He said

Dwellings of the Undead

Jayne Mansfield was deeply involved in the
blackest of the occult arts at the time
of her death in 1966. Here, Jayne receives the
satanic ritual communion with Anton
LaVey, head of the Church of Satan. (Anton LaVey)

Top: Clarkson, Tennessee abounds with legends
of strange lights in the sky, ghosts,
hauntings and a terrifying death. Even after
100 years, the unhappy ghost of Mr. Smoot
still walks the farm following his gruesome
death by a pen full of frenzied hogs. (Richard Winer)

Bottom: National Park Service employee, Jeremy
Leathers, felt a chill in the air. What had
first been only a slight drop in temperature
turned to icy cold. Yet, the air around
him felt still and warm. The gray mist was
concealing someone or something unknown at the
Stone River Battlefield in Tennessee. (Richard Winer)

As the magic of night transforms Hampton House's character, the haunters are once again its masters, prowling the dark hallways and grounds. Crashing chandeliers always herald the death of the first lady of Hampton. (Richard Winer)

Top: In the early morning hours, tormented screams echo through one of America's greatest shames—Hickory Hill. Only chains, shackles and a long-abandoned whipping post remain in that attic prison as painful memorials to the men, women and children who were tortured and died there; still, the disturbing sights and sounds persist. (George Sisk II)

Bottom: In the old jail in Tallahassee, weird noises originate from unknown sources. A séance produced evidence of life after death. (Richard Winer)

Wilder Tower at Chickamauga Battlefield is
where the strangest occurrence happened. One
evening, a fourteen-year-old boy climbed
to the top of the tower. Suddenly, a terrified
scream was heard inside. Panic-stricken, the
youth fled down the stairway and dived out
the wrong opening—down 25 feet onto solid concrete.
(Richard Winer)

Top: The Wedgewood Inn in New Jersey is
renowned in this world as a fine restaurant
and in the next world for bloody hands
that reach out of the walls. (Richard Winer)

Bottom: John Wayne's spirit still walks
the decks of his beloved yacht, the *Wild Goose*.
The new owner claims it is a very friendly
spirit. (Courtesy of Lynn Louis Hutchins)

The Hannah House was once used as a station in
the Underground Railroad prior to the Civil
War. Today, the upstairs rooms still reek
of decaying flesh and the bleak walls mask the
agonized shrieks of the long dead. (Courtesy of the
Elder family)

What untold horror pursues the Gray Lady
and what made her become an unhappy ghost at
historic Liberty Hall in Frankfort, Kentucky.
(Nancy Osborn Ishmael)

that he had strong feelings that he might not return alive. He gave away prized camera equipment, shook hands with his friends and colleagues and said a final goodbye. When questioned about his unusual behavior, he replied, "You don't understand. I won't be coming back." His friends were not aware that within days Brown would die filming his own murder.

Actually, it was another news photographer, Sammy Houston of Associated Press, who convinced Ryan to visit Jonestown. Houston and his wife Nadyne told Congressman Ryan what had happened to their son Robert, a one-time member of the People's Temple. "Our son would stand on the street corner and beg," said Mrs. Houston. Robert who was thirty-three, in addition to begging, "worked to exhaustion" holding down two different jobs as a railroad worker and a probation officer in order to keep up his two-thousand-dollar monthly contribution to Jones' Temple. Houston, who had been a member since 1969, was accused of breaking church regulations, and in 1976, he was found dead in the railroad yard only hours after breaking away from the Temple. When the cult moved, his widow was convinced by Jones to relocate with her two children to Guyana. Mrs. Houston would later accompany the Congressman to Jonestown in hopes of bringing her two grandchildren back to California.

Arriving in Guyana with his contingent of newsmen and aides, Ryan was not happy with his findings. Many People's Temple adherents wanted to defect. Families were divided—some members wanted to leave and others insisted on remaining. The congressman barely escaped injury when one of Jones' deranged followers attacked him with a knife. When Ryan, his party and some defectors left Jonestown for the Kaituma airfield some fifteen miles away, Jones sent a hit-squad to wipe them all out. Ryan and three newsmen were among those killed. Cameraman Brown kept his camera going until he was shot down. The developed film would show the murderers advancing toward their victims. But there were some survivors.

When word reached Jim Jones that the murderers botched the job and let a few of their intended victims escape, the cultists were all gathered together at the meeting hall where Jones was seated on his green throne. As a ring of his armed guards called "Angels" surrounded the congregation, a debate commenced after Jones told his followers of the killing of Ryan and some of his entourage. The subject of mass suicide was discussed. Mass suicide rites had been rehearsed previously by the commune. "Now, we must die with dignity," said Jones. "The GDF (Guyanese Defense Force) will question you. Then they will torture you. They will castrate you. They will shoot you. I can't leave any member of my family behind."

One of the commune members stepped forward and shouted, "I have a right to do with my life what I want, and you have no right to take my life away from me."

"I cannot leave you behind," replied Jones.

Residents began shouting and screaming, crying out to her, "Even if you don't want to die, you're going to die anyway. We will make you die!" Then the guards, armed with bows and arrows, rifles and pistols moved in and pushed the crowd into a tighter group.

"Now we must die and die with dignity," repeated Jones. He then commanded the nurses to prepare a powerful "potion" that was added to a large tub of strawberry flavored drink. "Bring the babies first," screamed Jones.

Babies were carried to the podium, and while still in their mothers' arms, their mouths were forced open and poison squirted inside. Some of the children were torn from the arms of hesitant mothers and dragged to the podium by guards or nurses. As the sobbing hysterical mothers watched, their babies went into painful spasmodic convulsions and died in minutes.

Then, the previously much practiced "white night" suicide ritual started going contrary to earlier rehearsals as the first victims retched and twisted in horrible pain. A number of the cultists, realizing that it was not another rehearsal but the real thing, began resisting and refused to willingly drink the poisoned beverage. Guards and other members had to hold them down while the liquid was forced down their throats. Some of the stronger resisters were injected with the poison as were those who didn't seem to be dying fast enough from ingesting the solution. Screams of agony and torturous moans echoed through the complex as the dying lay on the ground writhing with insufferable pain. Seeing his followers experience such a torturous death, Jones decided that he, himself, would die quicker and with less pain.

When authorities, who had been alerted by the few survivors who managed to escape the deadly ritual, arrived at Jonestown, they were appalled by the already decaying bodies. Many of the dead were contorted in agony. But not Jim Jones, for he died quickly—from a bullet. The final body count reached nine hundred and twelve, but that did not include those who managed to break free into the surrounding jungle only to succumb to deadly snakes, scorpions, piranhas, quicksand and whatever destruction the forest primeval had to offer. Also, the count didn't include those in Congressman Ryan's party who were murdered at the airfield. The bodies lying as many as thirty-three deep were so badly decomposed that limbs were falling off. Infestations of maggots and other crawling vermin moved in and out of mouths and other body orifices of the corpses. Guyanese policemen who'd witnessed death as a daily routine retched and vomited. When they attempted to move the bodies, pieces of rotted flesh and even limbs fell off in the hands of forensic team members.

Even after the bodies, or what was left of them after days of rotting under the equatorial sun, were taken away by gas-masked body-removal teams of the U.S. Army, the stench of death still remained suspended in the air at Jonestown. Jones' blood stains around his green throne and podium remained no matter how much effort was exerted to remove them. As perplexing as authorities found the unremovable blood stains, they were even more baffled by the discovery of the gun that killed Jones. The weapon was found in a building some distance away from the area where Jones' body was located.

Did Jim Jones succumb to cowardice when it came his turn to die? When he screamed to his flock to "die with dignity," did he exclude himself? There's no way Jones could have taken his own life, placed the gun where it was found and then returned to the podium area where his body was discovered . . . That is if it was indeed Jim Jones' body. But Army graves registration technicians who fingerprinted the cadaver said that the prints were definitely those of Jim Jones of the People's Temple.

If it was Jim Jones' body, then who is the figure resembling him whose presence has been seen on a number of occasions roaming the edge of the jungle surrounding Jonestown? A former government minister of Guyana stated, "Many people here in Guyana believe Jones had a double and that the real Jim Jones is alive." However, police officials and their men assigned to guard Jonestown are satisfied that Jones is dead. If so, then, again, who is the Jim Jones-like form seen near the commune perimeter?

A Guyanese police corporal, who had seen Jim Jones many times before the Jonestown day of death, has reported seeing Jones or Jones' ghost on at least three separate occasions. "He never said anything. His face had a strange cruel snarling smile. It was terrible."

An exorcism-like rite was performed at Jonestown by a minister and things seemed to settle down—for awhile. But then the apparition of Jim Jones was being sighted again. And there were more cries and moans of dying people coming from somewhere—either in the jungle or in the compound itself. "Animals in the night," say some. But others who've spent a lot of time in the jungle say, "No animal sounds like that." Is the ghost of Jim Jones condemned to roam forever in the jungle area of Jonestown? And have the souls of his flock become the cult of the undead, forever haunting the haunter?

Who or what is responsible for a number of deaths among persons involved with the People's Temple both directly and indirectly. The murders of William Duke, a Guyanese charter boat captain, and William Smith, another Guyanese citizen, have both been linked to the hidden loot of Jonestown. Duke apparently found some of the church's money and was crossing the Cuyuni River in an attempt to reach Venezuela with his find. He never made it, for his body was found floating face down, and there was no trace of the money. Smith also was linked to the treasure, and he was hacked to death while on the way to exchange some Jonestown dollars.

Mike Prokes, a Stockton, California television reporter who was a spokesman for Jim Jones, gave a most spectacular press conference in March of 1979, at which he read from a five-page defense of the cult. "I've got no martyr complex, but I refuse to let my black brothers and sisters die in vain."

Prokes, 31, then got up and walked from the motel conference consisting of eight photographers and reporters into the bathroom. The members of the press heard the sound of running water, and, then, the shattering blast of a pistol shot.

Rushing into the bathroom, they found Prokes lying on the floor, his tear-clogged eyes clouding over.

Three hours after firing the 32-caliber bullet into his head, Prokes died at a local hospital.

Jeannie Mills, who was a member of Jones' cult for six years before breaking away, wrote a book called *Six Years with God* which told of life inside Jones' People's Temple. She and her husband, Al, formed an organization in 1978, called The Human Freedom Center to help defectors from The People's Temple and other cults. Some members of the organization feared that "hit squads" had been organized to kill them after the Jonestown massacre. The Millses, too, feared the "hit squad." Mills was a pseudonym used by the authoress and her family for security reasons. Their names as cult members had been Elmer and Deanna Mertle. Jeannie Mills' fear of the Temple's hit squad was not unfounded. She told friends that her family was at the top of the list and that she feared Jim Jones could still carry out revenge from beyond the grave. On February 26, 1980, Jeannie and Al Mills and their fifteen-year-old daughter, Daphene, were shot to death in their Southeast Berkeley, California home.

What is this absorbs me quite?
Steals my senses, shuts my sight,
Drowns my spirit, draws my breath?
Tell me, my soul, can this be death?
Alexander Pope
("The Dying Christian to His Soul")

11

Roaming Spirits

In most cases, reported hauntings occur at the site where the entity suffered trauma, rather than at the site of his death or his grave. However, in the case of Mr. Perry C. Smoot, traumatic suffering, a gruesome death, and burial occurred at the same site.

Clarksville, in Montgomery County, Tennessee, is a small town located on the peninsula where the Cumberland and Red rivers of Tennessee meet. It is best known for tobacco processing and being the nearest city to Fort Campbell Army base, ten miles north on the Kentucky border. Clarksville abounds with legends of strange lights in the sky, ghosts, hauntings, and other bizarre happenings. But the death of Mr. Smoot is terrifying.

In the years just prior to the Civil War, there were a number of Yankees and Yankee sympathizers living in northern Tennessee. As war became apparent, many of them fled to the North, because of the way they were being treated. Many just packed what they could carry in one or two wagons and headed north, abandoning all other property and real estate. Others, like the Wheatley family, left a caretaker or overseer in charge of their farms. The Weatley farm, located north of Clarksville and about three miles south of the Kentucky state line, was left in the charge of Perry C. Smoot, an elderly bachelor who had no apparent political ties. When the Wheatleys left Oaklands, as their farm was called, Smoot moved into their house, where he lived alone. The slaves lived in an outbuilding. Although the Wheatleys were politically aligned with the Union, they still owned some slaves, for the Civil War erupted not over the issue of slavery but to prevent the southern states' secession from the Union.

Smoot was a harsh overseer who worked the slaves long and hard. He kept to himself much of the time and thus had few friends. Once a week he drove into Clarksville for supplies, but he had little social contact with the townsfolk. Apparently, they were unhappy that he was taking care of a Yankee-owned farm.

One day when he returned from Clarksville with a load of supplies, Smoot discovered that the Wheatleys' slaves had fled during his absence. By the time a posse was formed, the slaves had escaped into Kentucky. Smoot did what chores he was able to do by himself, but most work was left undone. He gave preference to feeding the cattle, horses, and hogs.

Clarksville fell to the northern armies early in 1862, and many runaway slaves returned as freed men. Although livestock from most farms in the area was confiscated, Oaklands was spared because its owners were Yankees. Still, Smoot did not make a secret of his dislike of the Union occupation troops. The troops in turn had little use for him. The returning slaves hated Smoot for the way he had treated them. Many neighbors and townspeople felt that Smoot was a traitor for looking after a Yankee-owned farm.

The night of December 16, 1862 was cold and blustery. A light snow was falling. Most of the Union troops occupying Clarksville had left to join General Rosecrans' Army of the Cumberland in the march to Stones River and Murfreesboro.

Because of the number of Confederate guerrillas who

managed to penetrate the Union lines, federal patrols had been stepped up. One of those patrols was passing by Oaklands on the night of the sixteenth when they heard horrifying screams followed by the raucous squeals and grunts of hogs. The soldiers rushed to the source of the commotion.

When they reached the log-built hog pen, one of the troops held a lantern over the edge. The appalling sight that met their eyes was more gruesome than anything they'd ever seen in battle. The hogs were in a frenzy, tearing apart the remains of a human being. The little of Smoot's body that was recoverable was deposited in two wooden buckets. The bloodied remains were then buried a few feet from the hog sty.

It was never ascertained how the sixty-year-old Smoot fell victim to the hogs. Did he lose his balance while feeding them? Did an angry neighbor give him a push as he leaned over the rail? Could it have been a former slave mad with vengeance or an irate Union soldier who shoved him into the pen?

Many folks in northern Montgomery County believe that the unhappy ghost of Perry Smoot still walks the farm. Some have recently seen the flickering light of his lantern floating along the path to the hog pen. Others have not only seen the light but have heard the victim's tormented screams in the night.

Does he haunt Oaklands because he was viciously murdered and can't rest until the crime is solved? Or is it possible that his spirit roams because he's upset that the remains of his shredded body are buried in a manure-filled cow pasture?

When night approaches and no inviting light can be seen for miles in any direction, screams emanate from the edges of darkness along with anguished cries for help, and a floating kerosene lamp is seen, held by a spectral hand. In the nearby house, now vacant, the restless spirit of a young woman is seen standing at an upstairs window. Was Smoot, supposedly a bachelor, actually married? Or might something have happened between him and a young woman that ultimately led to his death in the hog pen?

A half mile across the state line, in Christian County, Kentucky, a few hundred yards north of Concord Church, another apparition has been seen. The road, once a busy thoroughfare, is seldom used today, although it is not more than a few hundred feet from Interstate 24. The first report of a manifestation at that location was made by the late Dr. Robin Ferguson.

One night during a blizzard, Dr. Ferguson heard someone pounding on his door. It was a black man seeking the doctor's help for his wife, who was experiencing a difficult childbirth.

There was a foot of snow on the ground when the two men, both on horseback, started out for the man's house seven miles away. The snow had stopped falling and a nearly full moon gave the landscape a winter-wonderland effect. About halfway to their destination, they started down a long hill. As they neared the bottom of it, they saw a man standing in the snow about a dozen feet from the edge of the road. At first they thought it might be a hunter or a wayfarer. But when they got closer, they saw that the man was dressed in formal evening attire—top hat, tails, dress shirt. They also noticed that they couldn't see his breath, although the temperature was in the twenties.

As Dr. Ferguson was about to greet the stranger, something—a gut feeling—told him not to. He and his companion merely nodded as they passed the stranger, who nodded back in a congenial manner.

A little farther down the road, the doctor's companion leaned over in his saddle and said, "Dr. Ferguson, that wasn't a man. That was a ghost!"

The doctor replied, "Let's just keep riding, and don't— I repeat don't—look back." They continued riding until they reached the man's house.

After making sure that the mother and newborn child were all right, Dr. Ferguson left for home at daybreak. When he passed the place at the foot of the hill where, earlier, he'd seen the formally attired stranger, he saw nothing. No new snow had fallen since he had last passed the spot. Yet, the doctor could find no footprints or any other indication that someone or something had been there.

Others have also reported seeing the phantom party-goer. However, the road is so seldom used that there are no current reports concerning the formally attired manifestation. Is it possible that the old road is so little used today because of the *grande* ghost?

About twenty miles south of Clarksville is the small community of Pleasant View. Don Lewis, a studio cameraman at Nashville's WSM-TV told of some strange goings-on in his Pleasant View house, which was built in 1857.

"Shortly after we moved in," he said, "my wife told me, 'I know you're going to think I'm silly when I tell you this, and I know we're living in a very old house that's new to us ... but somebody keeps watching me. I can hear them breathe.' I told her that it was just drafts, which are common in old houses.

"This feeling of being watched and hearing strange sounds continued until finally she wanted to come to work with me at night. I work nights. She was too scared to stay home alone at night, even with the kids there to keep her company. At that point she was more nervous than terrified. Then something happened that really frightened the daylights out of her.

"One Sunday afternoon, Peggy was sitting by one of the big, long windows, knitting an afghan spread. We were trying to remodel the place, and I was doing some carpentry work. The window she was sitting next to was closed. There was no wind outside—it was calm. The room was semidark. She was just sitting there when she heard her name being called: 'Peggy, Peggy.' Then suddenly the curtain just billowed out and completely engulfed her. It couldn't have been caused by a breeze, because the window was shut. The only other explanation would be a draft from the fireplace. I checked the fireplace and found the dampers closed. I turned back toward Peggy, and I could tell that she was really terrified.

"I asked if she was sure she had heard her name called. 'Yes, I clearly heard them say, "Peggy."' When I asked her who said it, she replied, 'Whatever moved those curtains spoke my name.' As we were talking, the curtain billowed out again like a parachute, right in front of me. I saw it. Peggy wouldn't go into that room anymore."

(That room had originally been the parlor where family members were laid out for viewing when they died.)

"How long had you lived there when you first realized the house was haunted?" I asked.

"We've been living in the house three years now, and things started happening two weeks after we moved in. I can make the spirits, or whatever they are, come back. It seems that whenever I start remodeling the house, they start up again."

"Don, you keep saying 'they.' Is there more than one entity in your house?" I asked.

He nodded. "One is a small boy. It began in my daughter's room. There was the sound of a ball, like a basketball, being bounced. I thought my son—he was thirteen at the time—had gotten out of bed in the middle of the night and was dribbling a basketball around. Peggy was already awake and she grabbed my arm and said, 'You hear that, don't you?' I told her that I did, then I hollered my boy's name. But he didn't answer, and the ball kept bouncing.

"I got out of bed and started upstairs, calling his name again real loud. This time he answered, and I could tell he was in bed because the sound of his voice came from his bedroom, which is at the top of the stairs. When I walked into his room, he was half-asleep.

"About then, my little girl, who was nine at the time, called out to me. Meanwhile, the ball was still bouncing. I assumed that if it wasn't my son, it must be my daughter. So I went on to her room, where I found her hiding under the covers. When she heard me call, she pushed the covers away. As soon as her head popped out from under the covers, the sound of the bouncing ball stopped.

"She said, 'Daddy, can I sleep with you? Somebody's bouncing a ball, and every time I come out from under the covers, it stops. When I put my head back under the covers, it starts again.' I asked her to show me, and she did, but nothing happened. But I still believed her, because I heard the ball, too, and anyway there was no large ball in the house. I guess it was this incident that really made me believe all the things my wife had been saying.

"Later on that week, I worked all day long at restoring the house, tearing off and replacing siding and logs—the house was originally made of logs. After a hard day's work, I just plopped into bed. About two in the morning I was lying with my back toward the bedroom door when I heard something coming down the stairs. I assumed it was my son. I rolled over and said, 'Son, is that you?' There was no answer. I looked toward the door and saw this form. But as I stared at it, the thing vanished. At first I thought my son was playing tricks on me. I jumped out of bed, feeling upset with him, and as I walked toward the door I said, 'Son, what are you doing in our bedroom?'

"When I got to the doorway, I realized that no one was there. But I had no sooner gotten back into the bed when I heard this shuffling of feet on the stairs again. I turned over and saw a little guy about four feet tall. He looked like a little kid and was wearing what I thought was a night shirt or a man's white shirt.

"It was a small boy, and it definitely wasn't one of my children. He didn't seem to have substance. I could see every detail of his appearance, but he was somehow transparent.

"When I first heard his feet shuffling, he was about ten feet into the room. As I jumped up and looked at him, he ran back out into the hallway. But when I turned on the hall light, there wasn't anyone there."

"Could you tell anything about his hair style?" I asked.

"No," answered Don, who by then had tiny beads of sweat forming on his forehead, even though the lounge seemed overly air-conditioned. "He had on a hat, sort of a cap, but it was long like a night cap."

"Did the spirit of the little boy appear to walk, or did it seem to float out—how did it move?" I asked.

"It didn't walk *or* float. It jumped out of the room like any normal kid would. But everything was so dreamy— like now you see it, and now you don't. It was there. I know it was there. Nothing was wrong with me. I hadn't even had a beer. Both my children have heard the ghost and felt its presence.

"My wife and I talked about it. We realize that the old place is our home, but it's theirs [the ghosts'] too."

"When you researched the house," I questioned, "had there ever been any other reports of hauntings?"

"Our neighbors say there have been. One woman who lived in the house was reported to have lost her mind. The neighbors say she died in what is now my son's room."

I then asked Don when most of the hauntings occur.

"Mainly in the winter, seldom in the summer. As far as I can tell, it begins in the fall."

"How do your children react to the problem?" I asked.

"Well, my son wakes up sometimes at two or three in the morning. I find him sitting on the edge of the bed in a trancelike condition. He's not quite awake, but he's not asleep either. When he gets like that, he's like a sleep-walker. If I try to get through to him, he becomes very defiant."

I asked Don if his son reacts like that only during the winter months.

"Yes. My last sighting of the little boy was last winter, and my son's reactions seem to occur mostly during the times when the ghost is around. We have two dogs, Buffy, a poodle, and Peanut, a Scotch terrier, and sometimes they run upstairs as fast as they can go, yapping all the way. When they get to the top of the stairs, they start whimpering and yelping, then come running back down with their tails between their legs. Buffy looks back up at the darkness and really starts barking. There's nothing up there when I check it out, but there's a feeling as if someone or something is watching."

"What was the last occurrence that you and your family experienced in that house?"

Don straightened up in his chair and, looking directly at me, replied, "About two months ago, in June. Peggy and the kids were sitting on the couch, watching TV. The couch is in the middle of the room with a closed door behind it. Suddenly it was as if a capsule of cold air had been put over her, and she felt the presence of somebody trying to get through to her. She got up and took both kids into the kitchen. But it followed her there. She sat down and the cold air settled around her again. That's when she called me at work. She was crying and begged me to come home. I laughed at first. but then I realized that it wasn't funny. I told her to get hold of herself because she had the children to think about.

"One day last year, I got the same feeling, like being surrounded by a cold air mass. It was Indian summer— the last warm day or two before winter. I was in the yard making homemade ice cream. I felt a chilling sensation pass through my body. I also had a strong feeling of being watched. I looked around—it was still broad daylight—and when I glanced up at the window of my daughter's room, I saw a figure standing there, looking at me. As I watched, it moved away from the window. I suppose it disappeared because it saw me watching it. My daughter saw the figure too, and ran into the house and upstairs, but she couldn't find anything or anyone.

"Shortly after that, a neighbor gave us a twelve-inch-tall plaster statuette of a bride and groom that she said had belonged in the house many years ago. My wife placed it on the mantel. Shortly after, she saw a figure standing in the hallway. Before she had a chance to tell what it looked like, she was distracted by the statuette falling from the mantel. When she looked back toward the hall, it was empty."

The Lewises have decided against any attempt at exorcism, and continue to share their home with the ghosts of the past.

Dear as remembered kisses after death,
And sweet as those by hopeless Fancy feign'd
On lips that are for others; deep as love,
Deep as first love, and wild with all regret;
O Death in Life, the days that are no more!

Tennyson
("Tears Idle Tears")

12

A House of Things That Were

"No other house in Ohio is so steeped in myth and gruesome legend. No other house in Cleveland has evoked more curiosity or more sightseers," wrote Barbara Dreimiller, an Ohio writer.

Franklin Castle is an eerie, sixty-foot-tall structure of dark, gloomy stone. Even during the gaslight era it was considered a spooky place. Architectural experts describe it as being of Romanesque Revival style. There are over thirty rooms in Franklin Castle's four stories. The roof is a cluster of dormers and gables. Disguised sliding panels hide secret passageways. Supposedly, in one of these hidden passageways a thirteen-year-old girl was murdered by her father because he thought she was insane.

In the gloomy front tower, a bloody ax murder once took place. Some recent owners found a long-lost cupboard space still in use—a holding chamber of human bones. Whether the bones were placed in the cubicle by Hannes Tiedemann, the German immigrant who built the mansion in 1865, is not known. Deputy Coroner Dr. Lester Adelson, who examined the bones shortly after they were found in January 1975, said, "The human from whom these bones came has been dead for a long, long time. They are dried out and fragile to the touch." Tiedemann's fifteen-year-old daughter, Emma, and his eighty-four-year-old mother, Wiebeka, died in the house within a few weeks of each other in the winter of 1881. Tiedemann listed his daughter's cause of death as diabetes. Two years later, three small children in the Tiedemann family died in the building. The victims supposedly died of illnesses but suspicious neighbors felt that there was "more to the deaths than what met the eye."

To help take her mind off the tragedies, Tiedemann's wife, Luise, engaged the services of Cudell and Richardson, a prominent architectural firm, to design additions to the house. It was during this expansion that the secret passages, concealed rooms, and hidden doors were incorporated into the house, and it began to look like a castle. Gas lighting was installed throughout the structure and some of the fixtures are still visible today. A large ballroom, running the entire width of the house, with a fourteen-foot ceiling was included in the expansion project.

Today, guests are greeted by the face of a smiling child, chiseled out of stone, over the front entrance. But there are other greeters too, for even recently neighbors have reported seeing a mysterious "woman in black" staring down at them from the front tower room in which the bloody ax murder occurred over a hundred years ago, when Tiedemann was master of the manor.

John Webster, a Cleveland radio-station executive, investigated the house for a radio special on the hauntings of Franklin Castle. "When I was researching the house for the program," said Webster, "I was climbing the stairs, with a large tape recorder strapped over my shoulder, when something that I couldn't see tore the recorder from my shoulders. I just stood there holding the microphone as I watched the tape-recorder flying down to the bottom of the stairs, where it broke into pieces."

Mary Romano, whose husband at one time owned the house, found the dwelling terrifying. When her children played on the fourth floor, they were often joined by "ghost children." The day the Romanos moved into the castle, in January 1968, one of their two sets of twins went upstairs to play. A little while later, they came back down and asked their mother if they could have a cookie for their new friend. They said a little girl was upstairs crying. When Mrs. Romano followed the children back upstairs, there was no sign of another little girl. Could the ghost child be the spirit of one of the three Tiedemann children who died there around 1883, when there were five separate deaths in the house during a brief span of two years?

Mrs. Romano said that a Catholic priest had told her that the original owner, Mrs. Tiedemann, takes possession of her at times. "At times I feel as if I am not myself. It's very hard to explain, but I feel that someone else . . . I don't think I can describe it. The priest told me to pray for her to leave, but I didn't, because I was afraid to. I've been told that there are many entities in the house. The priest feels they are all evil. He feels I should get out of here, because they'll all affect me badly. I told him that the spirits have been very good to me—they've kept me from falling down the steps when others have been pushed. He told me that the spirits are very good to you until they get you in their grasp, and then they become evil and make you do evil things."

When a group of psychic investigators from the Northeast Ohio Psychical Research Society, an organization that has investigated more than 150 "haunted" houses in the area, sent a team to check out Franklin Castle, one of its members fled the building in terror.

Two of Mrs. Romano's sons from a previous marriage were living on the third floor. Something kept pulling the sheets from their beds. The boys packed up and moved out.

In September 1974, the Romanos also bailed out. They sold the house to Sam Muscatello for thirty-four thousand dollars. Muscatello had planned to make the castle into a church, but instead he sold guided tours through the building. But he too had problems with ghostly encounters—strange sounds from unknown sources, things vanishing, the young girl in black. In fact, it was after hearing Webster's radio special that he began to search behind panels and walls. He was the one who found the cupboard full of human bones. Apparently the grisly discovery had its effect on Muscatello, for he lost thirty pounds in a matter of weeks. Muscatello was never very successful in making Franklin Castle a tourist attraction. Whether the haunters had anything to do with it is not known.

Muscatello sold the house to a doctor for eighty-five thousand dollars, and in April 1979 she in turn sold it for the same amount to its present owner.

According to Barbara Dreimiller, who has spent considerable time investigating the building, the third floor is where most of the hauntings occur. "I was showing three friends about the house. When we reached the third floor, we saw a vapor or foglike object directly ahead of us. My friends stopped, but I continued walking toward it. I couldn't hold myself back. It just seemed to draw me on. When it engulfed me, I felt like I was breathing anesthesia. I just seemed to be drifting off into some kind of dream world. I couldn't resist. Just as I was passing out, my friends grabbed me and pulled me free from the thing.

"By the time I was fully conscious again, it had disappeared. We checked the entire room, but we could find no source or cause for the mysterious vapor.

"Another time, we were sitting in the servants' quarters, talking. I was admiring the wainscoting when suddenly a door in the wall virtually flew off and landed about eight or ten feet away."

Dreimiller also told of a certain spot on the third floor where, when some people stand on it, they experience an increased heartbeat and a shortness of breath.

Whatever is going on in the house on Franklin Avenue in Cleveland, there is no doubt that when *Cleveland Plain Dealer* newspaper referred to it as "the haunted castle," there had to be a real reason for the description.

*She died in beauty—like a rose Blown from its
    parent stem;
She died in beauty—like a pearl dropped from
    some diadem.*

Charles Doyne Sillery
(*She Died in Beauty*)

13

Ghosts of Liberty Hall

Mouth wide open, eyes dilated in terror, a beautiful
young woman runs wildly through the formal gardens of
Liberty Hall. A silent scream is frozen forever on her lips
as she streaks down the pathways as if pursued by the
devil himself. Jet-black hair blown about by a spectral
storm accents her bloodless white face. Drops of rain,
seemingly from nowhere, appear to spot her pastel satin
gown. What untold horror pursues her, and what made
her become an unhappy ghost at an old Georgian manor
house in Frankfort, Kentucky?

After an illustrious career of twelve years in the United
States Senate, John Brown* retired to Liberty Hall, his
magnificent estate in Kentucky's capital city.

John and Margaretta Brown lived and entertained roy-
ally in their mansion. Historically prominent men such as
Thomas Jefferson, George Washington, John Adams,
and James Monroe were frequent visitors. The great
French patriot Lafayette, Andrew Jackson, and Aaron
Burr were entertained there.

---

*No relation to the abolitionist.

Liberty Hall was named for the academy that John Brown attended in Virginia, which was established by his father, the Reverend John Brown. That institution is known as Washington and Lee University.

The structure was built on a "full-blown Georgian plan" with rooms flanking a huge central hall. An ornate grand stairway at the back of the hall leads to the second floor. The building was begun in 1796 or '97. Thomas Jefferson made suggestions regarding architectural design, but it is believed that the construction was well into its final stage when his comments were received. Today, Liberty Hall looks basically the same as it did when John and Margaretta lived there with their children.

Margaretta was an intelligent woman and a respected member of her church and her community. But she was often melancholy and withdrawn. One such period of depression occurred after the death of her eight-year-old daughter, Euphemia, in 1814. It is suspected that her death was caused more by the medical treatment she received than by her illness. Physicians of the time used huge doses of poisonous drugs to treat every ailment ranging from dandruff to scarlet fever. After the death of Euphemia, who is reported to have been an extremely gifted child, Margaretta discontinued the gay parties at Liberty Hall and refused to engage in any such frivolities again.

In happier times, about 1805, a reception was in progress for a beautiful soprano from New Orleans. It was a hot, muggy midsummer evening. Not a breeze stirred. From the magnificent formal ballroom of Liberty Hall came the soft strains of waltz music. Men and women, dressed in the height of Colonial fashion, whirled clockwise around the room. The rhythmic rustle of taffeta and fine silk, the shuffling of feet, and the soft murmur of voices punctuated by frivolous laughter echoed throughout the magnificent manor. The odors of perfume and perspiration, combined with the oppressive heat, created a heady atmosphere. "Yes," Margaretta Brown said to John, "you were right, my dear. It was an excellent idea to have the affair indoors. Not a blade of grass is moving outside. One of our frightful summer thunderstorms is in the making."

"Undoubtedly, my love," he answered. "And we wouldn't want our lovely houseguest Madame Rosa, drenched."

Both John and Margaretta glanced casually in the direction of the dark, beautiful young woman. "I see you've lost none of your love for beauty during your grueling political career," she replied, laughing lightly. "Your taste has much to recommend it. Madame Rosa's Latin temperament and appearance stand out strikingly."

The Spanish beauty was billed theatrically as Madame Rosa. She had never doubted her destiny to become a great opera star. The trip upriver by flatboat from New Orleans had been a difficult and dangerous one. But it was worth risking attack by marauding bands of Indians to be presented at Liberty Hall, which vied with the sophisticated glitter of the finest homes in Louisiana. One would never expect such opulence to be found in the Kentucky wilderness. But no matter, she thought, for the world would soon recognize her great talent.

A nearby mirror caught the reflection of her petite figure in a tightly corseted ball gown. She wore her hair piled high on her head, as was the fashion of the day. Gazing toward the mirror, Rosa brushed a strand of raven-black hair from her face. A flawless olive complexion accented her yellow silk gown.

But the hot, humid air and her tight corset left her feeling breathless and faint. As the clock struck midnight, Rosa walked unsteadily from the ballroom, down the stairs, and through a door that opened onto a beautiful garden . . . and into eternity, for it was there that she disappeared that night, never to be seen again—as flesh and blood.

Madame Rosa's absence was soon discovered. When a servant was sent to find her, he reported to the Browns that the opera singer had disappeared without a trace. An anxious citizenry searched through the morning hours in vain, for not one clue to her disappearance was discovered.

The gardens of Liberty Hall slope down to the banks of the Kentucky River. It was theorized that a prowling band of Indians was traveling along the river and, attracted by the laughter, lights, and music, followed the sounds of merriment and discovered the young woman alone in the garden. Then, possibly, they took her down-river and vanished into the wilderness. But why did her screams go unheard, and why were no signs of a struggle found?

Another theory is that most ghost sightings are reported on hot, sultry nights before a lightning storm, when barometric pressure is low and there is considerable electrical activity in the atmosphere. Are those conditions the most conducive for narrowing the gap between the world of the dead and that of the living? Is it possible that Madame Rosa, by some fluke of nature, was instantly transported into another dimension?

The incident left the citizens of Frankfort speculating for some time after the beauty's disappearance. One humid summer night, a frightened woman was seen running madly through the Browns' gardens. Thereafter, reports came in sporadically, concerning a horror-stricken ghost having been seen flying from an invisible pursuer. The description of the terrified specter matched that of the missing woman.

To my knowledge, Rosa's ghost was last seen in the summer of 1968. But few people want to talk about the ghosts of historic Liberty Hall. A former employee at Liberty Hall stated, "One morning I found a complete set of out-of-style women's clothing neatly stacked in the garden. But I didn't call the police. You don't do things like that at Liberty Hall."

Mrs. Robert H. Coleman recently retired from her position as curator of Liberty Hall after serving in that capacity for sixteen years. An interview with Mrs. Coleman was arranged by the Colonial Dames.*

"There are many accounts of ghosts at Liberty Hall," she said. "But the one most often reported is the Gray Lady. Over the years, visitors told many garbled stories about seeing strange things. Then my curiosity got the best of me and I began checking back into the records. I

---

*A philanthropic organization named officially The National Society of the Colonial Dames of America in the Commonwealth of Kentucky. That organization has administered the affairs of Liberty Hall since 1956. Its president is Mrs. S. C. Perry. She is also president of Liberty Hall, Inc., a nonprofit corporation. The Colonial Dames restore and preserve homes of historic interest.

found that the ghost has been seen by many people over the last 150 years. I started collecting accounts of what the spirit looked like. By the descriptions and first-hand accounts from folks who had seen the ghost, I not only discovered who it was but why the entity haunted Liberty Hall.

"Margaretta Brown's mother died when Margaretta was a small child, and her aunt, Mrs. Margaret Varick, finished raising the two children. After Margaretta moved to the backwoods of Kentucky, her letters home must have often seemed troubled and lonely. For in 1816, Mrs. Varick made the long trip from New York to Liberty Hall to be with Margaretta for a time. She was completely exhausted when she arrived, and she died a short time thereafter, apparently of a heart attack. She was buried in the family cemetery in the backyard at Liberty Hall. In 1845, her body was moved, along with the rest of the family's remains, to the big Frankfort Cemetery up on the hill.

"Since her death in 1816, the stories of Mrs. Varick's appearance in the house have been told and retold. People who have slept at Liberty Hall have awakened in the night to find themselves being tucked in by a peaceful-looking, quiet, smiling person wearing a long gray silk dress. And the spirit is helpful, too. Sometimes a quilt has been folded and put away, a window washed, or a bit of mending finished. Her story has become an integral part of the house, and a more harmless and gentle spirit could scarcely be found.

"Many have said that her spirit is at rest now that she's buried in the Frankfort Cemetery, but Mrs. Varick still makes her presence known."

"Is there any mention of ghosts in the volumes of correspondence you've researched at Liberty Hall?"

"Yes. The Gray Lady is mentioned in letters by various members of the Brown family who have seen her. The Brown family owned the mansion and grounds from the time it was built until the Colonial Dames started its administration in 1956. There are many files of letters dating back over a hundred years, and one in particular is very interesting. A girl from St. Louis was visiting there and wrote her father-in-law, saying, 'Why didn't you tell me there was a ghost at Liberty Hall? You let me come here and get scared out of my wits!' The woman was obviously furious."

"Is it true that you have a photograph of the Gray Lady?" I asked.

"Yes," Mrs. Coleman replied. "I took pictures of different stages of the restoration work. One day the man who developed my film called me, sounding very excited. On one exposure, coming down the stairs from the second story was an unmistakable likeness of a human figure."

I asked to see the photo. It appeared to be genuine. It's difficult to believe that the developer would take the time and trouble to create a fake ghostly image of the Gray Lady. The photograph is strong evidence of the existence of the Gray Lady. But there is other evidence, and other haunters, too.

"Other things must be taken into account," Mrs. Coleman continued. "One day, three gold bracelets seemed to materialize at Liberty Hall.

"It was winter; bitter cold and sleet had made the roads nearly impassable. We hadn't a single visitor in weeks. I went to Liberty Hall that day and made my usual check on things. There on a table, in plain view, were three gold bracelets. Thinking that perhaps the Dames had been there, I called all of them. The reply was always the same: 'No, I haven't been to Liberty Hall in a month.' To this day, no one admits owning those bracelets. There's just no explanation for them. And there are no stories of people hearing the jingle-jangle of bracelets in the house. Visitors have heard all kinds of sounds but not the jingling of gold bracelets."

"Were they real gold?" I asked.

"One is solid gold and the other two are gold-plated. I took them to a jeweler, who told me they were very old and were made in New York City about 1800. Mrs. Varick came from New York. They're still upstairs in the mansion, in the drawer of a small table. I guess that's where they belong."

"Has anyone investigated the hauntings at Liberty House?" I asked.

"Yes. There was a young man from Yale University who visited Liberty Hall for six weeks. He wanted to stay the entire phase of the moon to see if moonlight was somehow causing the sightings of the image of the Gray Lady in the upstairs window at night. The investigation proved that moonlight wasn't responsible for the sightings.

"For six weeks he had been trying to stay awake at night hoping to see a ghost. But he saw nothing. Toward the end of his stay, he gave up and fell asleep. Then something woke him in the middle of the night and he looked up. Standing by his side was a woman in gray. He said, 'Oh, Lord! Please, not now!' Then he turned his head into the pillow and went back to sleep.

"Another student who came to the library quite often to study was sitting in there one day poring over his books. Suddenly every hair on his body stood on end. Sweat started running down his face. But he didn't look up, just kept his eyes on the book in front of him and said, 'Gray Lady, I'm not ready for you yet.' He very quietly stood up, keeping his eyes focused on his shoes, and slipped out of the library and down the stairs to my office. He was as white as a sheet. Then he sat down in a chair beside me and said, 'I wasn't ready for her. I wasn't afraid, but I wasn't ready to look at her either!' "

"Somehow I got the impression that the Gray Lady was a nighttime ghost," I said, "but apparently that's not the case."

"The Gray Lady has been seen at all times of the day and night by hundreds of different people," Mrs. Coleman said.

"There was a big fire back in 1966, and Liberty Hall would have burned down if the flames and smoke hadn't been discovered right away. It was terrible. The fire gutted the hallway and destroyed some beautiful old things before it was extinguished.

"A man who worked for the *Frankfort State Journal* and a man with the local fire department stayed for three nights to protect the place from vandalism. They said doors would mysteriously close behind them and candles had a way of snuffing out when strange gusts of cool air suddenly came up. In an article for the *Journal,* the newspaperman wrote, 'I don't know the answers, but there's something weird going on in that house!' "

"Are there any other spirits haunting Liberty Hall?" I asked.

"There's a soldier who fought in the War of 1812," but it's just another ghost—nothing spectacular. One summer a young girl was visiting Liberty Hall. Her boyfriend had joined the Army to fight in the War of 1812 and was killed at the Battle of the Raisin—that's a river where the bloodiest battle of the war took place. But the soldier comes back to Liberty Hall, apparently hunting for his girlfriend. He comes in the back door off the porch and looks in each room as he goes down the halls, then he shakes his head, walks out the door, and disappears. He has been seen dressed in a dirty, bloodstained uniform. The soldier is evidently quite young, has blond hair, and looks pretty grimy and tired. I have no name for him."

"Are there any other peculiarities about the house?" I asked.

"The library door shuts by itself," she answered, "and there's a rocker that rocks all by itself. I finally put it upstairs. It rocks very briskly, and it's something you can't get used to, because it can be heard all over the house. I've checked for loose floorboards and things of that sort, but I haven't found anything. Many times I've gone upstairs to find it still rocking away—all by itself."

Mrs. Coleman then suggested that I get in touch with Byron Crawford, who had done a special program about the ghosts for WHAS-TV in Louisville.

After the interview with Mrs. Coleman, I stopped at the Frankfort Cemetery in search of Mrs. Varick's grave. High on a hilltop with a panoramic view of the Kentucky River valley are buried the remains of the Brown family. And they are in good company, too. Nearby, marked by an impressive monument, Daniel Boone lies beside his wife Rebecca. Countless other famous Americans rest in that ancient cemetery. But the Gray Lady did it again. I searched diligently but could not find her grave. However, I was assured by a local historian that Mrs. Varick's body does indeed lie somewhere on the hillside but that perhaps the grave is not in the Brown family plot.

I then contacted Byron Crawford, who has been a media personality and journalist for more years than he cares to say. His beat has been the back roads of Kentucky, and he has become somewhat of a modern-day folk hero along the foothills of the Cumberland. Following is Byron's account of the night he spent at Liberty Hall:

"Liberty Hall seems to have a personality, an intangible life about it, despite the fact that no one's lived there for years. It's the kind of place that makes you want to look back over your shoulder when you walk down the hall."

The muffled drum's sad roll has beat
The soldier's last tatoo!
No more on life's parade shall meet
The brave and fallen few.
On fame's eternal camping ground
Their silent tents are spread,
And glory guards with solemn round
The bivouac of the dead.

Theodore O'Hara
("The Bivouac of the Dead")

14

Battlefield Ghosts

The ranger felt a chill as the blackness of the night gave way to the light of a full moon. He knew the sudden chill wasn't from the night air, for he was warmly dressed. The path led him down a slight grade. At the bottom he saw a bank of swirling ground fog that he'd have to pass through. He had walked that route hundreds of times before and had gone into the fog on a number of those occasions. But this time, something was different. What had at first been only a slight drop in temperature turned to icy cold that seemed to penetrate through to his bones. Yet, the air around him felt still and warm. The shivers, he knew, resulted from his gut feeling that the gray mist was concealing someone or something unknown.

Then he saw the creature as it emerged from the fog. The shape was humanlike, but the ranger knew that it wasn't human. As the form approached, he tried to avoid looking directly at it. When less than twenty feet separated them, his eyes were irresistibly drawn toward the thing.

"When it passed me," said park ranger Edward Tinney, "I could see his hair was long like a woman's. The eyes—I'll never forget those eyes—they were glaring, almost greenish-orange in color, flashing like some sort of wild animal. The teeth were long and pointed like fangs. It was wearing a dark cape that seemed to be flapping in the wind, but there was no wind. I didn't know whether to run, scream, or what. Then the headlights of an approaching car came blazing through the fog, and the thing disappeared right in front of me."

It is not the strange and bizarre happenings that bring thousands of tourists flocking to Chickamauga Battlefield National Park each year, although a few of the visitors are aware of "Old Green Eyes" and its ghostly compatriots that stalk the grounds at night. Nearly 125,000 men fought at Chickamauga from the morning of September 18, 1863, to the night of September 21, when the vanquished began their retreat northward toward Chattanooga. For three days, the tide of victory swept from side to side in this, the bloodiest battle of the Civil War. Each side suffered twenty-eight percent casualties. Many Civil War scholars consider this battle, which took place a dozen miles south of Chattanooga, even bloodier than those at Antietam, Chancellorsville, and Gettysburg. It was the greatest southern victory of the war. General Braxton Bragg's Army of Tennessee drove General William Rosecrans' Army of the Cumberland back to Chattanooga, where they remained under siege, virtually cut off from the rest of the northern forces, until the middle of November, when a relief force led by General Grant broke through.

Chickamauga National Military Park is the oldest and largest of such military or battlefield parks. It is peaceful and tranquil now. The songs of birds and the sounds of gentle breezes blowing through the cedars give one a feeling of relaxation. But after the sun goes down, there no longer exists a feeling of contentment.

"Old Green Eyes is what we call it," said Edward Tinney, the supervisory park ranger and chief historian at Chickamauga. "The Chickamauga area has come to be associated with the macabre. Many corpses of Union soldiers lay where they fell for two months before they were buried. Thirty-four thousand men fell in seventeen hours."

"What or who is Old Green Eyes?" I asked.

"There are two legends concerning Old Green Eyes. The most popular is that a Confederate soldier had his head severed from his body during the height of the battle. All that was found to bury was his head. The rest of him was completely blown away. On misty nights, he roams the battle site, moaning pitifully, searching for his body.

"Visitors often see two frightful, glowing green eyes advancing toward them and hear an agonizing groan."

"Two different people in two different accidents," added Charlie Fisher, a ranger at Chickamauga, for the last twenty-four years, "totaled their cars against the same tree in the early 1970s. Both parties said they'd lost control when they saw old Green Eyes. I've never seen him myself, though."

"I've seen Green Eyes," said Ranger Tinney. "You know he's watching. We all know he's watching us. It's enough to make the hair stand up on the back of your neck—and I'm not a superstitious man."

"Mr. Tinney," I said, "you mentioned that there were two legends of Green Eyes. What is the other one?"

"The other one is that Old Green Eyes roamed these parts long before the Civil War and that it was seen moving among the dead on the battlefield at Snodgrass Hill during a lull in the fighting one night. That's where some of the bloodiest fighting took place."

"Have you ever heard any strange noises on these grounds?"

Mr. Tinney got up and walked to the window. Standing with his back to us, he answered, "Many times I've heard things, and I'm not the only one. Maybe it's all in our minds. In an environment like this, it's hard to separate reality from fantasy. I've heard people moaning. I've seen bushes moving when there was no wind blowing. I've heard gunfire. Maybe it was folks hunting, but who goes hunting at two in the morning? But mostly we hear moaning and groaning—sounds of suffering. I've heard plenty of sounds of horses, but there are horses stabled out there, so that doesn't mean anything."

When I asked him where the dead were buried, he turned around and went back to the chair behind his desk. "They're buried everywhere. One report said they were buried head to foot like cord wood. One grave or box could have three or four bodies. There are lots of monuments but no grave markers. Allowing arm's length, shoulder to shoulder, and room for men's bodies, those who died here at Chickamauga would stand nineteen rows deep for four and a half miles. There were so many of them that some lay bloated and rotting for days before they could be buried. Even today, sometimes the park maintenance crew accidentally digs up a body.

"And, surprisingly, some of the corpses are fairly well preserved after so many years. It's almost as if the ground here at Chickamauga refuses to accept the dead, as if it were unhallowed ground. Actually, I believe it's the high iron content of the soil that preserves the bodies. And those that were buried in iron coffins are nearly perfectly intact."

Jeffrey Thomas Leathers is a ranger at the Stones River Battlefield near Murfreesboro. On occasion, the rangers are called upon to help out at Chickamauga for special events, such as the celebration in September 1978 for the 115th anniversary of the battle. At those events, a number of rangers and other park employees don Civil War uniforms as part of the pageantry. Usually, the men wear that attire for several days prior to the event, in order to get the "feel" of their roles. Sometimes they even camp out on the battlefield in those uniforms and cook the same foods eaten by the troops during the Civil War era. Their tents are replicas of 1863 government-issue tents. Modern sidearms are exchanged for muzzle loaders or early breech loaders. Everything is authentic, from cooking utensils to latrines.

Jeffrey Leathers related the following bizarre occurrence at Chickamauga:

"It was September 17, 1978. We were getting ready to help in the dedication of a monument to Bushrod Johnson, a Confederate general, the next day. It was very near the anniversary date of the Battle of Chickamauga. We were sitting around our camp about one in the morning, when we decided to slip into our uniforms, get our fifes and drums, and parade around to scare cars on the highway that runs through Chickamauga.

"We were marching down the service road, playing the traditional British 'Long March,' when we looked over and saw what we thought was fox fire* along the side of the road. We were looking at it, and then we heard a terrible agonizing moan. It was unmistakable. We all ran back down the road without looking back."

"Are there any other strange things happening at the battle sites?" I asked.

"A beautiful lady in a lovely white gown has recently been seen floating about the grounds. Legend has it that she's looking for her sweetheart, who was one of the more than six thousand men who were missing after the Battle of Chickamauga."

"A well-known minister told me that he saw a man on horseback riding at full gallop—without a head," Ranger Charlie Fisher added.

"What would you say is the eeriest thing that's happened at Chickamauga that you know of, Charlie?"

"I would have to say—and I think everyone else who works here will agree—that what happened in the Wilder Tower, the monument that marks the center of the Union lines where the southerners broke through, might be the strangest occurrence."

The Wilder Tower is a gray stone structure eighty-five feet high. It was erected in 1903 by the men who served under Colonel John T. Wilder. It was the colonel's mounted infantry, armed with Spencer repeating rifles, that held off the charging Confederate forces long enough for the fleeing Union troops to change their rout into an orderly retreat. When Wilder joined the service, the Union Army was so ill equipped that his men were given mules to ride and hatchets as weapons. After much political pressure, he and his men finally had their mules replaced by horses. But hatchets were still their weapons, except for the few men who had their own muskets. So, at his own expense, Wilder bought each of his troops one of the new Spencer repeating seven-shot rifles. He purchased 2,100 of them for thirteen dollars each. Because of the

---

*A phosphorescent light given off by rotting wood.

repeating rifles, which were the only ones at Chickamauga, Wilder's 2,100 men were able to hold back
14,000 screaming Rebels long enough for their fleeing
comrades in blue to organize an orderly retreat. One can't
begin to guess how many Yankee soldiers were saved that
day by Wilder's men.

The tower was erected in Wilder's memory by the
survivors of his mounted infantry. Souvenirs of the Civil
War were sealed in the cornerstone of the structure.
However, when officials went to open the cornerstone as
part of the bicentennial activities in 1976, they found the
stone apparently undisturbed, but upon opening it they
discovered the contents missing. Yet, there were no traces
or marks to indicate that the vault had been tampered
with.

Ranger Fisher told us about the bizarre occurrence at
Wilder Tower:

"It was back in 1969 or '70—a dark, moonless night.
The Wilder Tower has an observation deck on top. Because the park is open to the public, we have to lock the
tower at night. Well, a fourteen-year-old boy pulled himself up the lightning rod that was on the back of the
tower. Then he reached the first gun slot,* about fourteen
feet above the ground, and entered the structure. After he
got inside, he ran up the 136 steps to the top and called
to some friends who were drinking beer about fifty feet
from the tower. Suddenly, the people down below heard a
terrified scream inside the structure. Panic-stricken and
confused, the youth fled down the winding stairway. He
had come to what he though was the same opening through
which he had entered, and practically dived out through
the narrow slot—but it was the wrong slot. He fell head
first on the solid concrete twenty-five feet beneath. Although he survived, he's completely paralyzed for the rest
of his life. He could never explain what it was that horrified him."

After receiving permission to stay on the park grounds
that night, we drove our truck to the campsite near

---

*A gun slot is a long, narrow opening, less than twelve inches wide, that
was used to aim a rifle in order to fire upon the enemy.

Snodgrass Hill. Around midnight, we decided to take some night photographs of Wilder Tower, showing what it looked like when the boy had his unfortunate fall. After shooting both color slides and black-and-white pictures of the drab, gray stone structure, we drove back toward our campsite. Upon passing Snodgrass Hill, we decided to park, climb the hill, and prowl about the various monuments dedicated around the turn of the century by veterans of the many different outfits that fought there. Although it was eerie, we found nothing strange or unusual, except that the night seemed much darker than normal.

We returned to camp about two in the morning and were bedding down when we heard gun shots that seemed to be coming from Snodgrass Hill. We went back there but found nothing. All was silent. Only later would we find out that we were mistaken.

The next morning we headed for the Stones River Battlefield National Park near Murfreesboro, Tennessee.

The ghostly soldiers who haunt Stones River Battlefield National Park today are real, according to the rangers and Park Service employees who have seen them. "There are still strange things happening here," said Jeffrey Leathers.

"The park has a number of tourist stops with plaques commemorating the Civil War action that took place at a particular stop. Stop number four is a rocky, wooded area with a number of sinkholes. You never hear birds there, and it's always ten to twenty degrees colder than the surrounding terrain. Metals like guns or cannon will sweat cold water in that hollow. Sometimes, especially after ten at night, you can hear something or someone following you when there's no one behind you.

"During an anniversary of the battle here at Stones River, my friends and I were camped out in the woods. We were walking down in that hollow one night and heard some footsteps following us. When we turned around we found nothing. We even checked the underbrush. This has happened three times. The last occurrence was near the end of December 1978, on the anniversary of the battle.

"On another occasion, several of us were camped out

by Stop Six. I woke up about three in the morning, craving a drink of water. My canteen was empty, so I started for the administration building. It was foggy. As I was passing some cedars, I noticed what looked like a man standing or hiding in the bushes. I thought it was one of the guys playing around, so I yelled for him to come out. He raised one hand and started toward me. I told him to stop, and he raised the other hand and kept coming. I always carry live rounds in my cartridge box. Well, I loaded a live round and said, 'I'm going to give you one more chance. Stop, or I'll fire.' About that time, he seemed to fall right into the ground, and I couldn't see him anymore. When I got to where I had last seen him, I could find nothing—not even a footprint or broken twig.

"The Shiloh Battlefield was the site of another bizarre occurrence," Leathers continued. "There was a man we called Mr. Minnie Ball. The rangers had been trying to catch him for a long time. He'd been digging up Civil War relics in the park, and that's illegal. He'd use a metal detector to find whatever he could and then sell the artifacts at a good price. There are bodies buried everywhere at the battlefield sites—unmarked, of course. So, to dig anywhere on the grounds of Shiloh is the same as grave-robbing. And it's against the law.

"One night some rangers were patrolling the woods and they came across a smashed metal detector. About a hundred and fifty feet away, at the edge of the woods, they found a man sitting in a car. He seemed to be in shock. He wouldn't move or respond in any way. They took him to a hospital but he never would talk about what happened. Eventually, he had to get psychiatric help, and the conclusion everybody came to was that he, Mr. Minnie Ball, encountered something in the woods that scared him out of his mind. I was told that while digging up a grave and robbing some buttons from the corpse, a bony hand came up out of the grave, grabbed the buttons from his hand, and yanked them right back into the ground."

Ron A. Gibbs is Chief of Interpretation and Resources Management at Stones River. The best description of his job would be that of historian. He is also a supervisory ranger.

According to Gibbs, there are many unexplainable things happening at our Civil War battlefield parks. Shiloh, which was the scene of one of the war's bloodiest battles, is a typical example. "Every battlefield has its ghost stories," said Gibbs. "Probably some are merely myths, but I'm sure there's more than just a grain of truth to most of them.

"The only strange thing that I've actually experienced myself is the cold, strange feeling at tourist Stop Four. Now, my wife, well . . . let her tell it."

Pat Gibbs, sitting on the couch next to her husband, began her story. "My husband and I were walking through the middle of the park. We were going from glade to glade. As we emerged from the woods into an open area, I looked at the row of trees beyond and got a very uncomfortable feeling. The closer we got to those trees, the more uncomfortable I felt.

"I had chills and became very tense. The feeling kept growing more until I actually started shaking. We reached one point where I stopped and said I didn't want to go on. The emotions were fear and panic, and it was very, very intense. It was real. I repeated to Ron that I didn't want to go into the next wooded area. When we walked into the glade anyway, I began crying.

"I knew something terrible had happened there, and I was experiencing it. But I couldn't tell what it was or why it was happening to me. There was almost a defined line, and I could step in and out of it. When we were in that area, I couldn't stop crying and trembling. It was like someone else's emotions possessed me. I was experiencing someone else's trauma, and it was centralized in one little hollow in the glade. The trees there are very old. We experimented and walked in and out of the area several times, and my reactions were always the same.

"We were in the area where Sheridan had held off a Confederate attack. But I had no details on what had happened. Ron took a friend of ours in there who is psychic. He walked into the area and said the reason I was feeling such intense emotion was that something awful had happened to a woman there, and it didn't have anything to do with the battle. He said it was a black woman, and he could see a building burning, and it had something to do with an ax. He thought a black woman was ax-murdered in that glade.

"Ron talked to some of the older black people around here and discovered a true story about a Ku Klux Klan murder. The Klan had terrorized a black community that once existed here. It was mispronounced 'Seminary' but was actually named 'Cemetery.' A black woman was raped and killed at Tourist Stop Four, where I picked up the vibrations. A schoolhouse had been burned. The black woman, a young schoolteacher, was taken from the schoolhouse by the Klan, assaulted, and murdered with an ax. Her only crime was her strong desire to educate black youngsters."

At Chickamauga, a manlike creature in the night, with fanged teeth and glowing orange eyes, that is called Old Green Eyes, appears out of the fog; at Shiloh, a skeletal hand reaches from a grave, and spectral soldiers still roam after being dead for nearly 120 years. These accounts are almost too incredible to believe. Yet, they've been witnessed by United States Government employees who have no reason to make them up.

There was the volley of gunfire at two in the morning on the darkest nights at Chickamauga, miles from civilization. And we personally experienced the clammy chill associated with cold spots in the ghostly glade at Stones River. But it took an unexplainable image on a color slide to finally convince us that there really are a lot more bizarre things happening at memorial battle sites than most people want to believe.

As described earlier in this chapter, we left our campsite at Chickamauga around midnight to photograph Wilder Tower. It was there that a teenage boy virtually threw himself head first out a window while in a state of panic. Using a pair of Nikon cameras with wide-angle lenses, we took three back-and-white shots on plus x and two Kodachrome color-slide pictures. All five pictures were exposed with a Sunpak Model 611 flashgun. Both strobe and cameras were set at full exposure. On close examination, the black-and-white tower pictures were perfectly normal, although slightly underexposed.

The color slides were normal too, but on each of them there was an obvious shaft of light beaming upward from the top of the tower, as though it were a lighthouse with an intense beam projected skyward. Yet, there was no light source within two hundred feet of the gray stone structure.

Could the light photographed atop the Wilder Tower be some form of energy mass? Why was it not visible to the naked eye at the time the pictures were taken, and why did it show up only on the color film? Even photographic technicians were unable to explain the image. Perhaps an entity from another dimension was attempting to communicate that the strange experiences of park rangers were more than mere ghost tales or figments of whimsical imaginations.

Due to the high escarpment upon which the house is built, the wind is an eerie banshee at times, whistling through the garret rooms. At night, so legend persists, the wind takes on strange voices, the lament of people chained in servitude.

Family Digest, May 1974

15

The Old Slave House

In the early morning hours, tormented screams and cries echo through the skeletal, stark gray edifice that once housed America's greatest shame—Hickory Hill. The sounds of agonized humanity do not belong to the world of the living but to the realm of phantoms. Only chains, shackles, and a long-abandoned whipping post remain in that musty attic prison as painful memorials to the men, women, and children who were tortured and died there; still, the disturbing sights and sounds persist.

Two Marines who saw combat in Vietnam volunteered to spend a night in the haunted house. It was not just a run-of-the-mill haunted house but a place of horror. When told that others who had attempted to spend a night at the Old Slave House near Harrisburg, Illinois, had fled in terror, they replied, "We're Marines. Just show us the way."

The two were growing bored in the garret of the Old Slave House. It was about one o'clock in the morning, and they'd been sitting there for hours. The only light in the third-floor room was given off by a kerosene lantern. One of the Marines yawned and was about to close his eyes, when the lantern began flickering. There were no drafts or other air movement. Then, suddenly a high-pitched agonized moan tore the silence. It seemed to come from every direction at once. There were sounds of people talking and other strange noises. Suddenly, swirling forms appeared out of the darkness that advanced upon them. Whistling, bansheelike screams, unlike anything either of the two jungle fighters had ever heard, shattered the stillness. Dozens of ghostly forms began moving around the room, nearly surrounding them. The Marines panicked. So, on a dark night in 1966 two members of the most elite of all U.S. fighting forces were routed by a sinister enemy and fled in terror.

In the early days of the Old Slave House, many African slaves and their descendants who had bought their freedom or had been emancipated by their owners came to Illinois. They worked the salt mines and the farms in Gallatin, Hardin, Pope, and Massac counties. However, many of them were only temporary residents. After escaping the hardships of slavery in the South by fleeing to Illinois, a "free" state since 1831, they were transported by means of the Underground Railroad to safer territories farther north.* Thus, children of former slaves were born in freedom. Life in the so-called free states was not easy, but the young ones had never known the cruelty of overseers or felt the sting of a whip across their backs. Manacles had never bound their wrists; shackles had never restricted them as they worked or played.

Then, bands of night-riders known as "Regulators" swept across Illinois and became the law of the land. The black children were easy prey. The crimes of the Regulators were so evil that even the usually apathetic white community was outraged. Black children were kidnapped from their freed families and were taken to Alabama and Kentucky, where they were auctioned as slaves. Freed black adults were occasionally kidnapped and sold back into servitude. Those who were sold as slaves in the South were the lucky ones, for many of the unfortunate blacks abducted by the Regulators found themselves prisoners of John Hart Crenshaw.

The front page of a newspaper in Equality, Illinois,

---

*Antislavery groups organized a secret system of helping runaway slaves escape their masters. It was known as the Underground Railway.

dated July 27, 1829, carried the following article, under the byline of Leo D. White:

"HORRID OUTRAGE! Was Kidnapped, in the neighborhood of the Saline, a NEGRO GIRL, named MARIA, about eight years of age, dark complexion, nearly black, well grown of her age. She was taken from the spring on Saturday evening of the 25th by two ruffians who are unknown. This girl is one of the negroes emancipated by the last will and testament of John McAllister, of Montgomery [sic] County, Tennessee, and moved here about a year ago, and some time last spring some scoundrel—probably one of these—stole two horse creatures from them, and thereby prevented them from making a crop, and now returned to steal the children. The uncle of the girl, a black man of the name DRYAS, offers a reward of FIFTY DOLLARS for the girl, and a subscription is now making up for the Girl and Thief or Thieves, and I am of opinion that TWO HUNDRED DOLLARS will be raised."

While Uncle Dryas was putting up his life savings for the safe return of his niece, the people of Equality cried out against the heartless "thieves" who had kidnapped Maria. They were unaware that, in all likelihood, Maria was being held captive by John Hart Crenshaw, a highly respected businessman and pillar of the church and community. She was probably being held prisoner behind barred doors in the fetid breeding chambers on the third floor of Crenshaw's mansion. There waited "Uncle Bob," an uncle of a different sort from anything she had yet known.

Uncle Bob was one of John Crenshaw's southern-bought slaves. He was a physical giant of a man, chosen because of his intelligence, size, physical stamina and virility. Uncle Bob had been selected primarily for stud service. However, Crenshaw cannot be credited entirely with originating the concept of genetic engineering. An effort had also been made in Lyon County, Kentucky, to selectively create a superior strain of slaves. Breeding sturdier slaves wasn't the only thing compelling Uncle Bob onward to higher levels of productivity. On the southern slave market, a pregnant black woman or a black mother with an infant was worth two hundred dollars more than a female without a child. Crenshaw

sold as slaves any adult servants or children on hand in
excess of his needs. That practice turned a tidy profit on a
market where healthy slaves sold for as much as eight
hundred to a thousand dollars. It is believed that Uncle
Bob sired no less than three hundred babies to be sold
into slavery in a span of ten years—to his knowledge.
And who should know better than Uncle Bob himself!
Uncle Bob, who soldiered for the Southern Army during
the Civil War, died as recently as 1949 at the Elgin
Veterans Hospital. No one knew the exact age of the
former slave, but he had to be more than 114 years
old.

Uncle Bob's owner, John Hart Crenshaw, was a grand-
son of John Hart, whose signature appears on the Decla-
ration of Independence. As a young boy, Crenshaw saw
his family home in New Madrid, Missouri, destroyed by
the great earthquake of 1811. William and Elizabeth Hart
Crenshaw, John's parents, took the family to Gallatin
County, Illinois. The Crenshaws settled near a salt well
called the Half Moon Lick, on Eagle Creek. William
Crenshaw died shortly after the move, leaving his eldest
son, John, to provide for his mother and six brothers and
sisters. When only eighteen years old, he worked full time
in the salt refineries. In 1817, he married Miss Sina
Taylor, and they commenced married life at the Crenshaw homestead at Half Moon Lick. Perhaps the back-
breaking work in the salt mines and the deprivations in
John Hart Crenshaw's early life drove him to the desper-
ate and willfully inhumane acts that eventually caused his
downfall.

There are natural salt deposits along the banks of the
Saline River in southern Illinois. Provision of men to
work the salt deposits was written into the Illinois State
Constitution of 1818 in Article VI, Section 2: "No person
bound to labor in any other State shall be hired to labor
in this State, except within the tract reserved for the salt
works near Shawneetown; nor even at that place for a
longer period than one year at one time, nor shall it be
allowed there after the year 1825. Any violation of this
article shall effect the emancipation of such person from
his obligation to service."

Many blacks and indentured whites earned their freedom by working in the salt mines according to the terms of the Constitution of 1818. However, the article that technically freed these slaves gave John Crenshaw the legal tool that made him a very wealthy and influential man. Slavery was outlawed in Illinois, but Crenshaw, acting under the terms of the Constitution of 1818, leased slaves from Kentucky and Tennessee to work salt miles that he had rented from the state. He became so wealthy that he personally paid one-seventh of the total taxes gathered in the state of Illinois. His land holdings were thought to be nearly thirty thousand acres. Leased slaves as well as kidnapped freed men and women worked Crenshaw's fields and salt mines. Although many saved enough money to buy their way out of slavery, Crenshaw rarely issued the customary Certificates of Freedom. The black slaves had no official voice, and therefore they were powerless to prevent or to protest the injustice done them.

Crenshaw's classic Greek plantation home still stands majestically on a windswept hilltop in southern Illinois, with a panoramic view of the Saline River valley and the Shawnee Hills. Its location near Harrisburg, Illinois, and the Kentucky border, made it a strategic site for dealing the slave trade. It has many unusual features designed by its owner to facilitate some of the most shameful atrocities ever inflicted upon Afro-Americans in this country. Presently known as the Old Slave House, Crenshaw called his mansion Hickory Hill. William Cavin, a noted contractor and architect, laid the foundation for Hickory Hill in 1834, but the structure was not completed until 1842.

The immense three-story manor house was built with twelve huge columns supporting the verandas, each cut from the heart of a single pine tree. While Crenshaw's neighbors dwelt in miserable one-room cabins and dirt-floor hovels, he and his family lived in opulent surroundings. All art work and furnishings at Hickory Hill had been imported from Europe, and each room was individually heated by a large fireplace.

The most interesting part of the Crenshaw mansion was the conveniently built carriage driveway within the walls of the house. Carriages loaded with illegal slaves were brought inside unnoticed. The human cargo was then deposited on the first floor and dragged up the back stairs to the infamous attic. On that floor are a dozen cell-like rooms with tiny windows facing onto the hall. A narrow corridor separates the two rows of stalls. Immense windows extend nearly from ceiling to floor at each end of the corridor, providing light throughout the attic. Prisoners were secured to heavy metal rings that hung from the walls of each cubicle. Only one room is different from the others—the breeding room that once belonged to Uncle Bob, which measures nine by twelve feet. Most of the rooms are not much larger than an average grave. The whipping posts still remain, where slaves were strung up by their thumbs and cruelly flogged. Heavy iron balls and metal shackles can still be seen. Many had been sized to fit children.

Crenshaw's imprisoned slaves had no rights by law, so they protested in the only way they knew how—with violence. Crenshaw, in collaboration with the Regulators, had kidnapped freed men, women, and children and had sold them into slavery. A jury of white men tried him for that crime, but, due to his political prestige and financial clout, he was declared innocent. Shortly before the trial, Crenshaw's steam mill was burned to the ground. But arson wasn't the first act of violence against Crenshaw. Once, when he was unmercifully beating a black woman in the fields, an enraged slave seized a broadax and severed his leg. That incident, however, only caused Crenshaw to intensify his mistreatment of slaves.

Ironically, just before the outbreak of the Civil War, Abraham Lincoln visited John Hart and Sina Taylor Crenshaw. Perhaps Lincoln was attempting to enlist Crenshaw's political support. And perhaps the time he spent at Hickory Hill strengthened his antislavery convictions, for no man possessed of compassion and sensitivity could have remained unmoved by the horrors occurring at Hickory Hill.

Crenshaw's profitable businesses eventually failed. Court actions against him, slave uprisings and the discovery of salt in Virginia and Ohio dealt the final blow to his enterprises. Deprived of the slave and salt markets, he resorted to farming his extensive land holdings until his death, on December 4, 1871. Ten years later, his wife, Sina, died at the age of eighty-two. In nearby Hickory Hill Cemetery rest the final remains of John and Sina Crenshaw—but do they rest? For it is said that "after candle-lighting time, you can hear strange sounds and whimpering coming from the upper room . . . and too at times you hear the soft strains of old Negro spirituals and the sound of Sina's organ hauntingly played."

Does the horror of such evil deeds ever die? Or can it live on in the dark garret rooms of the Old Slave House? I would soon find out, for I was on my way to investigate reports of a haunting there.

The Old Slave House stands high over the fertile Saline River valley. The distant Shawnee foothills are the only higher terrain in sight. From his aerie, John Crenshaw could have watched his servants labor in the surrounding fields as he selected victims for his cruelty. Evidence of a recently worked coal mine can be seen near a ramshackle old barn. A "gob pile" composed of a low-grade coal byproduct is clearly visible from the road. Bales of rolled hay and rusting farm equipment lined the steep path as I drove up Hickory Hill to interview Janice and George M. Sisk, II, and their ten-year-old son, George.

When I explained my purpose for visiting the Sisk family and the Old Slave House, Mrs. Sisk sobered for a moment, then invited me into the foyer of the mansion and introduced me to her husband, an athletic-looking man in his early forties.

"I've lived in the Old Slave House just about all my life," said Mr. Sisk. "This house has been in my family for more than seventy years. I was a year old when my parents came here to live, and my father was two years old when my grandparents brought him here.

"This place is important to us. If my family hadn't stayed and looked after the property, all this history would have been lost. We keep the Old Slave House open to tourists from April to the end of November."

When I asked about the hauntings, Mr. Sisk replied,

"The Old Slave House *is* haunted, and the earliest I can trace the stories back would be to this article from the Benton, Illinois, *Post-Dispatch*."

He handed me a yellowed newspaper clipping. Part of the date had been rubbed off through the years, but Mr. Sisk said that the story was written in the late 1920s. It read, in part: "Whether ghost chaser Hickman Whittington expects to see a white or a black ghost remains to be seen. He said he had recently learned that cries have been heard coming from the post where slaves were whipped for disobedience, and he intends to do something about it."

"What happened to Whittington?" I asked.

"Whatever it was, it scared the life out of him. He was an exorcist, but they called them ghost-chasers back then. When he visited this place he was in fine health, but just after he left here he took sick, and he died in a small town nearby just hours after his visit. . . . You might say something scared him to death."

"Mr. Sisk, what would you say that 'something' was? What could have affected Mr. Whittington so adversely that he died?"

"I wouldn't want to be the one to say. But it could have been the same thing that scared those two Marines that tried to stay in the attic overnight in 1966. But they had the good sense to leave before anything disastrous happened."

"What happened to the two Marines?"

"Who knows?" replied Sisk, shrugging his shoulders. "I only know that they came flying down those stairs about one-thirty in the morning. Said they saw forms coming at them. They were in a state of shock. I really didn't get to talk to them very long. They tore out of here in a hurry. Those boys didn't even bother to go back upstairs to get their belongings."

"A reporter named David Rodgers finally spent the night in the attic in 1978. Other reporters before Rodgers had tried to stay the night, but none of them made it. They all said they heard shuffling feet and whimpering cries in the slave quarters at night."

David Rodgers, the twenty-six-year-old Harrisburg reporter, had been the first to spend an entire night in the old slave quarters. "I was so exhausted fighting fears," he had said, "I was actually shaking. That place is so spooky. The tape recorder wasn't picking up the sounds I was hearing."

"Mr. Sisk, do you believe in ghosts?" I asked.

He looked at me strangely. "I don't believe in ghosts but I respect them. They were here before I was, and they don't do me any harm. I feel sympathetic. There has been so much suffering here, you know."

I then took my tape recorder and other paraphernalia into an adjoining bedroom, done in early American decor, where Mrs. Sisk and her son were waiting for me. Choosing a comfortable chair near a tea table, I began, "That old gray tree in the yard—it's really grotesque, with its root system exposed like that. It looks like a giant spider creeping toward the house. One might think it would wrap its tentacles around the old house and crush it some stormy night."

"Yes," Mrs. Sisk replied. "That old blue beechnut tree could be dangerous in a thunderstorm. But it's got quite a history, so we don't want to cut it down. It was brought here by John Crenshaw from the grave of George Washington. The tree was only a sapling then. The howling winds around the Old Slave House have exposed the roots, and the local teenagers haven't been able to resist carving their initials on it. The old tree can't last much longer, but then, nothing lasts forever.

"We have twelve rooms on the first and second floors," she continued. "There was a thirteenth room added on later. Good thing I'm not superstitious. There are twenty other rooms besides the thirteen, but they've been left unfinished. Those rooms are just the way they must have been when John Crenshaw lived here."

"Why weren't the other rooms converted into living quarters?"

"There was really no use for them. The first two levels more than adequately housed the people who lived here. Originally there were stalls on the third floor to imprison female slaves, but one of the former owners tore some of them out. You can still see where the nails and hinges were. Otherwise, the attic is just the way it was when Crenshaw had it built."

"How did you feel when you first came here to live?" I asked.

"I'll have to be truthful and say that the place always upset me. Actually, I left my husband in the early years of our marriage because of this house. I really didn't leave *him*—it was the house. I felt that the vibrations from the house were jeopardizing my physical and mental health. When I moved away, I weighed only ninety-five pounds, and it was due to dwelling on the history of what happened here and the strange things that go on all the time. Our son was fifteen months old when I left. I just had to get away from this house. It's so isolated, and there aren't any neighbors close by."

"What disturbs you most about the house?" I asked.

"Several things really get to me. The strange sounds bother me a lot. I can make excuses for some of them. I tell myself it's the wind. Now, over there," she said, pointing toward a huge window, "when the wind blows— at least I think it's the wind—I hear a sound just like a fog horn. It's loud, and it sounds like a boat going down the river. The kitchen window rattles—like a shrill little song. Since I moved back, I've become conditioned to both the explainable and the unexplainable noises.

"We can make excuses for those kinds of sounds—they might be caused by wind or by animals. But one night when we were lying in bed, I heard a loud crashing sound like glass breaking. Thinking that a window had broken, we got up to investigate. There was nothing broken, but there's no doubt that we heard the sound of glass breaking."

"Has anything happened to any of the visitors who come here?" I asked.

"Yes. We hear lots of stories, but there was one thing we witnessed ourselves. Frankly, I wouldn't have believed it if I hadn't seen it myself. A woman came running down the stairs one day, asking why certain peculiar happenings were taking place in the attic. We followed her up to the third floor. And this is God's own truth—she stood in one spot and the hairs rose right up on her arms! When she moved away from that spot, the hairs on her arms went down. She ran downstairs in panic. We hear a lot of these things from tourists. But that poor woman was frantic. She demanded to know why it was happening, but we couldn't give her a logical reason. Mostly, people tell us that they feel uncomfortable here. Some say they can actually slip back into that time period. The emotional reactions of the visitors are very strong."

"Have you or anyone else ever seen anything?"

"It's the same as the sounds around here. You learn to ignore what you think you see. Sometimes I see forms out of the corner of my eyes. They're just forms. I can't make out who or what I'm seeing."

"Have you ever had the feeling you're being watched or that you're not alone?"

"Living here in this house, with its antiques and its history, I think my husband and I both agree that we feel like we're being observed all the time. We never feel we're alone in the house.

"But, going back to the noises. Another sound that shook me up tremendously happened one night when I was lying here in this bed," she said, gesturing toward a large four-poster bed. "There was a loud sound, like something or someone banging from under the floor with a hammer. I heard it clearly three times. But what it was, I don't know."

"Did you ever try to investigate the noises?" I asked.

"At first we did, but not anymore. I know now that there's something here. It knows that I'm not going to do it any harm, and it hasn't harmed me in the ten years I've been here.

"It's three to six degrees cooler up here than in the valley, even in the summer. Maybe it's because there's nothing to protect this knoll from the wind," she said, in a half-hearted effort to explain the incredible chill at the Old Slave House. An anxious expression spread across her face, as if she was tired of offering excuses for the strange goings-on at Hickory Hill.

Are there any other things in particular that have frightened you?"

"Our bathroom is located in the back part of the house right off the dining room. When I try to take a bath in the evenings, I hear someone call out my name. It's so clear that I say, 'I'll be out there in just a minute!' thinking it's my husband. I hear a voice yell out, 'Janice!' and I run out thinking it's him, but he's not there. No one's there. No one's *ever* there. And it's only my name I've heard being called, no one else's in the family. I don't take baths in the evening anymore—just in the morning and when my husband is home."

Mrs. Sisk then turned to her ten-year-old son, George, Jr. "Go ahead, honey—tell him what you hang on your dresser at night."

The youngster hesitated before answering. "I hang a rosary on my dresser to keep the devil out of my room."

"Why do you think the devil is in your room?" I asked, watching the boy's face.

"Well, it's hard to put in words. But I believe the devil exists, just like I believe in Jesus."

"Is there any reason to believe the devil might be interested in this house?"

"There might be a chance," he said, "that evil spirits are in here. I sure hope not, but I'm not taking any chances. I've got the sign of the holy eucharist hanging over my bed just to make sure that whatever's in this house doesn't bother me."

"Have you seen or heard anything peculiar?"

"I've heard loud noises that sound like gunshots. Something hurt my dog, Pete, one time. But a cow might have kicked him—maybe. And it sure scared me when a picture fell off the wall right by my dad. It made a big, loud noise."

"This house has seen so much bloodshed and turmoil," said Mrs. Sisk. "Even the Crenshaw family, the original owners who had slaves here—all you have to do is look at their portraits and study the eyes. You can see that they are not happy people; you can see the bitterness and hatred, together with lust for power. I can see it when I look at their eyes."

"Have you ever considered having the house blessed or an exorcism performed?"

"Some people came through once and offered to do the ceremony. They said the house was 'heavy with phenomena.' But we decided that whatever's upstairs can stay up there. I believe in leaving things like that alone.

"Catholic priests have come here and told us that if we permit or encourage psychic things to go on in this house, the negative energy might enter into our bodies and possess us. I think that could happen. Sometimes I watch my husband's face and wonder if the spirit of John Crenshaw doesn't try to enter into him. His eyes seem to change at times, and it's as if I'm looking into the cruel, wild eyes of John Crenshaw."

The look of horror on Mrs. Sisk's face required no further comment.

I excused myself and slipped up the stairs to the slave quarters. The second and third floors of the structure are unheated, and the winds that whip around the house make it even colder. But as I ascended the last bare wooden stair to the slave detention and breeding chambers, a cold draft rushed past, chilling me to the bone. Yet, there were no windows open.

In the awesome silence, I tuned in to the vibrations of the past and opened psychic channels of my mind to spirit entities who have chosen to visit the mansion from other dimensions. Suddenly I was startled by a sound like an agonizing groan. Was it only the wind? I immediately received psychic impressions of frightened young black women who had been assaulted, cruelly punished, or had given birth in these cold, barren rooms.

From the farthest corner of my mind came the sound of footsteps on the stairs behind me. I wheeled around in the semidarkness, not knowing what to expect. It was Mr. Sisk. Breathing a sigh of relief, I invited him to join me. We found ourselves speaking softly in memory of the nameless slaves whose cries of pain went unheard. But I fear that the spirits of those who suffered so much on the third floor of the Old Slave House still bear their ordeals there, even as this is being written.

But why do I talk of Death?
That Phantom of grisly bone,
I hardly fear its terrible shape,
It seems so like my own—
Thomas Hood
("The Song of the Shirt")

16

Ghostly Theaters

Specters have long been associated with the world of the theatre; indeed, no other art form fosters so much superstition. And actors, with their vivid imaginations, are among the most superstitious of artists. Behind their outward show of confidence, actors, like the rest of us, experience tension, frustration, and anxiety. Because their profession affords success to only a relative few, aspiring actors must dedicate their entire lives to their work, in spite of the heartbreak involved. Thus, it stands to reason that after death, they might choose the theatre as their spiritual abode.

The best documented and most famous of all haunted theatres is London's Theatre Royal—better known as the Drury Lane. Its daytime ghosts, the Man in Gray, has been seen at morning rehearsals and at matinees, most often in the front row of the balcony. Sometimes he walks the aisles and vanishes through walls. He has been seen by stagehands, electricians, cleaners, and other members of the theatre's staff. Members of the audience have seen him and assumed that he was a member of the cast or a uniformed usher.

No one knows who the Man in Gray is or anything about him. He just appears and disappears, and has been doing so for more than two hundred years.

In 1850, alterations were being made to increase the theatre's seating capacity. When workmen knocked down a brick wall—one through which the Man in Gray had often been seen vanishing—they made a most grisly discovery. On the floor, amid a scattering of playing cards and gold coins, was the skeleton of a man with a dagger between its ribs. The unidentified remains were buried nearby.

That should have been the end of the ghost of the Man in Gray. But he continues to attend performances at the "Lane." Among the recent shows at which he was seen were *My Fair Lady; The King and I; No, No, Nanette;* and *Oklahoma.* It is believed that if he manifests at a rehearsal, the play is sure to be a success; if he fails to appear, the show usually bombs out—as was the case with *Plain and Fancy* and with *Pacific 1980.* One can imagine the distress of performers who fail to encounter the ghost by the time the final dress rehearsal ends.

There are a number of other ghosts at the Drury Lane. One has even helped actors dress for their performances. Another gives words of encouragement to nervous performers. And one has been known to kick or prod players who do a bad job of acting.

Several ghosts at the Drury Lane have been identified: Charles Kean, an actor from the nineteenth century, and Clifford Heatherly, who died in 1937. The latter's ghost actually appeared on stage during a performance, in front of both cast and audience.

Other noted English theatres claim to have "house" ghosts—the Adelphi, the Haymarket Theatre Royal, the Palace, the Gaity, the Piccadilly, the Duke of York, and more.

One of England's oldest theatres, the Margate, is reportedly haunted by the ghost of Sarah Thorne, who managed the theatre during the mid-1800s. She also founded a drama school there. Her spirit has shown both approval of and objection to various performances. She's most often seen floating down an aisle or one of the theatre's creaking wooden hallways.

On the other side of the Atlantic, on November 28, 1979, an auction was held at the Sotheby Parke-Bernet gallery in New York City. A total of 137 relics of Abraham Lincoln were sold. The famous president's top hat brought a high bid of ten thousand dollars. However, the top bid of the day was made by a representative of the *Forbes* Magazine organization, in the amount of twenty-four thousand dollars. That was the highest price ever paid for a piece of Lincoln memorabilia. The item was the opera glasses Lincoln was using at Ford's Theatre in Washington, D.C., on April 14, 1865—the night he was assassinated by John Wilkes Booth. Ford's Theatre is probably the best-known haunted theatre in the United States. Although Lincoln's ghost has never been seen there, the sale of his opera glasses spurred the erroneous legend that he haunts the theatre. The murdered president does haunt, however. His apparition has been seen at Springfield, Illinois, at Gettysburg, and by a number of dignitaries at the White House—but never at Ford's Theatre.

Booth forced his way into Lincoln's box, shot the president in the head, and made good his escape by leaping from the box down onto the stage. During the escape he broke his leg, but he managed to flee into the street. A famous Civil War photographer, Mathew B. Brady, took a photograph of the interior of the theatre. It revealed a semitransparent figure standing in Lincoln's box. Although the apparition was not too clear, it resembled Booth—who, incidentally, was a not-too-successful actor—more than it resembled Lincoln.

A few years later the theatre closed, and it remained empty for nearly a century. After years of disuse, in 1968 the Ford's Theatre Society began restoring the building as a showplace, theatrical museum and part-time working theatre. Phantomlike forms have been seen in the old playhouse, but none resemble Lincoln. Some claim it is the spirit of John Wilkes Booth. Regardless of whose presence it is, many persons have felt and heard it—stage curtains being raised and lowered when there was no one there to do it, mysterious footsteps, weird voices laughing and crying and even reciting, and lights unexplainably going on and off. While some of the people at Ford's

Theatre deny that anything strange is going on, others readily confirm that strange things do occur there.

Also in Washington, D.C., is the National Theatre. According to legend, it is haunted by the ghost of a murdered actor costumed as Hamlet. Supposedly he stalks the stage and backstage areas after the theatre has closed for the night. However, the phantom seems to appear most often on opening nights.

The National was financed by public-spirited citizens who felt that Washington needed a first-class theatre. The doors opened for the first time on December 7, 1835. In March 1845, President Polk held his inaugural ball there. The next night, the theatre burned down. It was rebuilt and reopened five years later, in time for Jenny Lind, the "Swedish Nightingale," to perform for President Fillmore, his cabinet, and Congress.

In the years that followed, the National was gutted by three more fires, and a wall collapsed during a circus performance. On April 14, 1865, President Lincoln had planned to attend a performance at the National. However, his wife convinced him that the play at nearby Ford's Theatre was better. Thus, the Lincolns attended the latter hall, and the course of history was changed.

One of Washington's old storm sewers passed through the basement of the National Theatre. It is said that some of the poorer actors washed their clothes there. The sewer, which was sealed a few years ago, ran directly under the stage.

The legend is derived from an incident that occurred in 1885. Two actors, while doing their laundry in the basement sewer, got into an argument. One killed the other. The victim, actor John McCullough, was buried by his killer in a small dirt area that can still be seen today in the cellar of the theatre. Although the murder was discovered, McCullough's body was never exhumed. However, the apparition that was seen at the National was recognized as McCullough by those who knew him. At first, actors were so startled when they saw the ghost sitting in the audience that they bungled their lines. Contrary to the legend, when McCullough's spirit was seen, it was not wearing a Hamlet costume—which could mean that more than one ghost stalks the National Theatre.

According to the manager of the theatre, in 1932 the police wanted to exhume the actor's remains. But the regular performers at the National protested. "He's an actor. He's buried in a theatre. What more could he want?" they said.

In 1976, an electrician, working on some wires in the basement near the spot where McCullough is supposed to be buried, uncovered a rusted gun from the Civil War era. Could it have been the murder weapon?

A retired stage doorman claims to have seen both the Hamlet-costumed ghost and McCullough's spirit on a number of occasions. The latter was always seen on opening nights, busying himself with making sure that everything was in order. It does appear that the National Theatre has a phantom "extra" standing in the wings.

Halfway across the country from Washington, D.C., is the Orpheum Theatre in Memphis. One of its regular patrons is named Mary. She usually wears a glowing white dress. Her faint footsteps can be heard as she glides down the aisle to her favorite seat, C-5. She looks to be about twelve or thirteen years old. But she's different from the other theater-goers, because she's been dead for more than sixty years.

Today, when legitimate theatres look more like college auditoriums, one is struck by the elegance and grandeur of preserved or restored old theatres. The Orpheum is one of these. It seems like a cathedral, with its huge rotunda-like dome and two-thousand-pound chandeliers. The maroon carpets and exotic tapestries are like something out of the *Arabian Nights*. The dome lights give an effect not unlike that of a full moon.

For many years it was thought that Mary was the ghost of a young girl who was killed in a 1923 fire in downtown Memphis. However, several years ago, a parapsychology class from Memphis State University conducted a séance at the theatre. The participants in the ritual found that the ghost did indeed call herself Mary. However, that Mary did not perish in the 1923 fire; she was killed in 1921 in some sort of falling accident not too far from the theatre itself. Apparently, she—or rather her spirit—wandered into the Orpheum, liked what she saw, and decided to stay.

Mary has been known to materialize in a number of different ways. A reporter who wrote a story on the Orpheum hauntings for *Memphis Magazine* vividly described his strange experience:

"I turned to speak to whoever it was that had been sitting next to me, and it struck me that there was nobody there. Yet, I had been sure of it just seconds before. Now I was getting confused. I looked around the theatre, trying to locate someone to talk to about what I had just felt. The entire theatre was empty. Everyone [he was a member of a group of thirteen who were ghost-hunting in the theatre at the time] was somewhere else in the lobby or perhaps, the storage rooms, the mezzanine, the balcony, the loge area—the theatre area itself was completely deserted. I started up the aisle; I had to find someone to talk to, to tell them about the weirdness down by the stage. I turned to tell the person behind me to hurry up—again it hit me, this time much more intensely. There was nobody there; yet, I had been so sure of it that I had actually turned to speak to them. As I entered the lobby, the things that I had just felt were almost immediately erased."

In 1977, when the New York company of *Fiddler on the Roof* arrived at the Orpheum for their Memphis engagement, they felt that the house was haunted and insisted that a séance be held in the balcony following their opening-night performance.

Other performing groups have also experienced the strange occurrences at the Orpheum. Some players have seen the little girl in her flowing white dress. Others have heard stage doors slamming when there was no one there to do it. They've heard footsteps in the balcony when they could see that it was deserted. Prancing shadows have been seen darting about when there were no lights or figures to account for it. At times the theatre is permeated with cold spots—even on hot summer days when the air-conditioning is off. One actor described it: "It sort of penetrates deep inside down to your bones—like being immersed in cold liver." Sometimes the huge organ plays by itself, no special tune—just random notes as if a child were attempting to play it.

Another man who has been associated with the

Orpheum for over a quarter of a century said that he never saw any ghosts there. But he did admit that strange things happen, like spontaneous organ music, stage lights going on and off, and stage curtains being raised and lowered when there is no one there to perform those things. There have been times when, after new lightbulbs have been placed high up in the dome, they wouldn't work the next day. Somehow, someone or something has gotten up into the dome and loosened the bulbs.

An electrician who works late at night in the theatre has heard a young girl singing, "a definite female soprano voice," in the empty theatre. Every time he went to investigate, the voice stopped.

A maintenance employee who has been doing restoration work in the theatre for years recalls one night when he was working alone in the building. He was holding a bunch of wires that he'd just finished coding and bundling when he noticed that the screwdriver he needed was just out of reach. Putting down the wires to get the screwdriver would have necessitated redoing all the wires. He explained what happened next: "It was a very minor thing, but it was something that would unnerve you. I looked back down and there was the screwdriver somehow lying at my feet. I said to myself, 'I don't understand this, I don't want to understand it. Thanks a lot, but this is a little bit beyond me.' So, I went down, and I left."

He also maintains the theatre's huge organs. "To this day," he claimed, "you can go up in that right-side organ chamber, and you'll get the strangest feeling that you'll ever know. And I don't know what it is."

Another maintenance man at the Orpheum reported that he saw a little girl running down the aisle. That same night, his key broke in the door as he was trying to get out of the theatre.

The Assistant Project Director for the Memphis Development Foundation, which owns and operates the theatre, has experienced "eerie feelings" in both the basement and the projection booth of the Orpheum. He has heard footsteps and seen shadows darting around the theatre when it was dark and empty.

The organist and former general manager of the Orpheum has his own feelings about the ghost: "Mary is mischievous, capricious, and rather childish. She's not doing mischief all the time, but when she does, it's usually in the form of a practical joke—like the lightbulbs in the dome being loosened."

In April 1979, a woman named Teresa spoke with a small group who stayed over late at the theatre. They were listening to the organist play "Never Never Land." Each time he played that song, the theatre became extremely cold. Some of the group watched a faint light bounce into the theatre from the lobby and disappear behind some seats in the rear. Teresa said, "I was scared to go into the lobby, because I knew something was out there. It was just an overpowering feeling." Finally, Teresa and two others ventured out to the lobby. The three saw "a little girl with brownish hair dancing in the distance." Teresa struggled against a compulsion to walk over to the little girl. "This was extremely frightening," she said, "because while my mind was telling me there's no such thing as a ghost, something was drawing me toward the spot where the little girl was. I started toward her but caught myself. It was like she was calling me. That really scared me, for I felt that if I went near her, I'd never come back the same."

Before the days of television, one could, for twenty-five cents or less, spend an afternoon in some of the most elegant edifices America has ever seen—the downtown movie theatre.

The lobbies of these theatres were incredibly opulent, with sculpted gold-colored columns a dozen feet in circumference, oriental-carpeted grand staircases, chandeliers twice the size of the ticket booths, bubbling fountains spewing crystal-clear water into fishponds carved from stone, elaborate, bigger-than-life murals, and hand-carved chairs and benches. But, like the streetcars that carried people to their doors, nearly all of these theatres have passed from the American scene.

The Syracuse Area Landmark Theatre—or SALT as it is called—is probably the most exquisite of any restored theatre. When SALT opened its doors for the first time in 1928, it was christened Loew's State. Its designer was Thomas W. Lamb, the world's leading theatrical architect of his day. Lamb considered Loew's State in Syracuse the most exotic and finest of the three hundred theatres that he had designed during his distinguished career.

To step from Salina Street into the lobby of SALT is to be transported into an Oriental splendor. SALT is the ultimate in magnificence and beauty. And it is haunted.

One night during the summer of 1977, just after the Syracuse Area Landmark Theatre group was formed to restore the old playhouse, a group of volunteers was cleaning up twenty years' worth of backstage neglect. The doors were locked to keep out anyone not affiliated with the restoration project. The workers noticed one of their group standing on the stage, his eyes fixed on the balcony. Then the others saw it too—a woman in her sixties dressed in a silver evening gown. The volunteers called up to the balcony, asking the woman what she wanted and how she had gotten into the building. She sat in an aisle seat, staring straight ahead and did not answer. Becoming irritated at being ignored, several workers started for the balcony stairs, but before they were even off the stage, the woman in the evening gown vanished before their eyes.

One of the members of the restoration committee contacted a local psychic. The psychic described the woman in the balcony exactly as the workers had seen her, even though no one had told her what the apparition looked like. The psychic went on to describe what she was picking up on the woman: "Either she or her husband was a former member of the staff of Loew's, and all her life this woman wanted to be an actress. But she got only a few bit roles, and she went to her grave a frustrated actress. Now she has decided to spend her afterlife in Loew's State Theatre. She's very glad that you people saved it."

The psychic also said that the woman in the balcony had sat with the board of directors when they were planning the restoration of Loew's State, and she put ideas into their heads that contributed to the success of the project.

On another occasion, the phantom woman was seen by a television crew filming a special about the haunted theatre. Before they could turn their cameras on her, she vanished—but not before hurling at them a spherical object enshrouded in fog, which vanished when it landed on the stage.

During the restoration, a sealed-off dressing room was discovered just off the downstairs ladies' room. It was a mirrored room complete with an art deco chandelier. The psychic was able to describe that dressing room before it had been discovered. Other psychics have found the area "very active." Several persons have reported seeing what they thought was the phantom woman's reflection in the mirrors in the dressing room. Others have seen flashes of light moving down the stairs leading to the dressing room.

*When I am dead and nervous hands have thrust
My body downward into careless dust;
I think the grave cannot suffice to hold
My spirit prisoned in the sunless mould!*

John G. Neihardt
("When I am Dead")

17

The Ghosts of the Dakota

At the corner of Central Park West and Seventy-Second Street in New York City is the bleak-looking Dakota Apartment building. Its architect, Henry Hardenbergh, described it as German Renaissance. Its builder, Edward Clark, who was the president of the Singer Sewing Machine Company, died in 1882, two years before the Dakota was finished. Construction time was nearly four years.

Almost until the turn of the century, the Dakota was surrounded by hog pens, grazing cattle, chicken coops, shanties, and squatters' shacks. Today, it is surrounded on three sides by concrete. To the east it faces Central Park. When completed, it was Manhattan's only multistory structure north of Fifty-Ninth Street and was the first luxury apartment building on the West Side.

It was originally to be called the Clark Apartments, after the builder. But the structure was so different from the other buildings in New York that it became known as "Clark's Folly." A friend commented to Clark one day, "You might as well be putting it up in Dakota Territory," referring to the fact that the building was so far from the hub of the city. Being a man of good humor, Clark changed the name to Dakota. The architect was told to incorporate Wild West details into the building's trim— arrowheads, a carved stone head of an Indian, bundles of wheat, corn, etc. Those, combined with stone gargoyles, and many other strange carvings, add to the structure's spookiness.

The Dakota is no longer restricted to the upper crust as it was for many years. In 1960 it was converted from rental apartments to a cooperative. Many celebrities have lived in the Dakota, such as Judy Holliday, who died there after a lengthy bout with terminal cancer; actor Robert Ryan, whose wife also died of cancer there; Jose Ferrer and his wife, Rosemary Clooney; Fannie Hurst; Jack Palance; Roberta Flack; the late John Lennon and Yoko Ono; Judy Garland; Lauren Becall; Betty Friedan; the Steinways of piano-manufacturing fame; and, of course, William Henry Pratt, better known as Boris Karloff.

Even without its hauntings, the Dakota has a wealth of interesting stories. *Life at the Dakota*,* by Stephen Birmingham, offers much insight into the building and its residents, and it even has a chapter on the ghosts of the Dakota. Birmingham writes, "One did not live at the Dakota long before it could be sensed that here was not an ordinary apartment house but a living breathing presence."

There were numerous happenings well in excess of the normal. For instance, all the fireplaces worked, but on many occasions the smoke from one fireplace would not spiral skyward out of a chimney but would drift into another apartment, even though each flue was separate and not known to connect to any other.

When the Novaks moved into the Dakota, they brought with them some rare parrots that they had owned for years. When they had bought them, they were told that the birds were unable to breed in captivity. But as soon as the Novaks moved into the Dakota, the parrots began laying eggs.

Back in 1961, one of the Dakota's four cage-type elevators simply vanished. No trace of it has ever been found.

*Random House, 1979.

As strange as the Dakota is, some of its occupants are just as unusual. Miss Leo owns an eighteen-room apartment in the Dakota and is the building's oldest resident (said to be in her late nineties). For many years she never set foot out of her apartment. Some years ago, when one of her favorite carriage horses died, she had it stuffed and placed it in her drawing room. The mounted horse was fitted with a full suit of medieval equestrian armor. Then a suit of human armor was assembled, complete with a lance, and was seated on the animal. Both horse and "rider" could be seen through Miss Leo's Seventy-Second Street window.

In the center of the building is an H-shaped courtyard originally used as a carriage turn-around. One of its entryways was an archway from Seventy-Third Street. This was originally the servants' entrance, but the servants complained that it was inconvenient. It has since become known as the "undertaker's gate" and is opened only for the removal of deceased residents of the Dakota, which occurs about once a year.

One apartment is rumored to have a thirty-thousand-dollar treasure trove hidden under the floor. It was supposedly placed there before the turn of the century. The apartment is now occupied by Yoko Ono.

Those are some of the strange and unusual things that have taken place in the Dakota. But there are ghostly things, too. For many years there have been rumors of eerie, ghostly happenings. Some people refer to the Dakota as the "Dracula," and many swear that the place is haunted.

After Judy Holliday's death in 1965, her apartment was bought by the Gary Smith family. When Mr. Smith first looked at the apartment, the walls were painted a dreary gray, the massive mahogany woodwork had darkened from many revarnishings, and the entire kitchen was painted black.

Three men were engaged to repaint the Smiths' new apartment. They went about their work, but after several days they began to have the feeling that they were being watched. Then one day a ghost appeared in front of one of them as he was working alone in one of the bedrooms. "It looked like a boy about nine or ten. He gave off an unusual outdoorlike odor—kind of musty-smelling. His clothes were from another era. He was wearing what you might call a Buster Brown suit. He stood there watching me paint, then wandered off down the hall."

One of the other painters also saw a ghost watching him work. But it was no longer a small boy; it had changed into a young man. Although the apparition's body appeared to be in its twenties, the face was that of a small boy. The painters saw the manifestation several more times.

When the repainting job was finished and the furniture was being moved in, a painter was standing on a ladder doing some touch-up work in a large closet. Suddenly the door slammed shut by itself and the light went off. After groping his way down the ladder and propping the door open with a chair, he switched the light back on and climbed back up the ladder. As he reached toward the ceiling with his paint brush, something he couldn't see grabbed his arm and pulled it tight against the lightbulb. He was so astounded that he just watched the hot bulb scorching his skin. It was a number of seconds before he was able to yank his arm away from the burning bulb. Yet, he felt no pain at the time or later, although a scar was left on his arm.

Jo Mielziner was the Dakota's unofficial historian until his death in 1976. He kept several scrapbooks on the building during the many years he lived there. After he died in a taxicab at the Dakota's main entrance, strange things began to happen. Tenant Wilbur Ross, a banker, was called to the basement by a porter who told him that a heavy snow shovel hanging on the wall had suddenly gone flying across the cellar, nearly striking him. The porter then told Ross why garbage was strewn about that part of the basement: "I had it all wrapped in plastic bags and stacked next to the service door, when the bags suddenly started flying around the place."

As Ross listened somewhat skeptically to the porter's story, a heavy metal bar came hurtling across the room and landed at his feet. He tried to lift it, but it was too heavy. Other tenants who experienced similar manifestations decided that they were the result of Jo Mielziner's not wanting to cross over to the other side.

A little girl with long blond hair, a yellow dress that looked as if it belonged in another century, silver-buckled patent leather shoes, and white stockings to her knees came bouncing a ball down a hallway where some painters were working. "It's my birthday," she said, as she passed them and disappeared down the hall. One of the painters who had worked in the Dakota for a number of years said he had never seen her before. The description of the little girl did not fit that of any child in the building, either resident or guest. To this day, no one at the Dakota knows who she was. Shortly thereafter, one of the painters to whom she spoke fell from a scaffold down a stairwell and was killed. The little girl with the bouncing ball was thought to be a harbinger of death.

Frederic Weinstein is a writer. He and his wife, Suzanne, have often heard footsteps and other noises coming from within the walls of their third-floor apartment. Although he isn't accident-prone, Mr. Weinstein has had a number of mishaps in his dining room, where the sounds of pacing back and forth are most prevalent. Rugs have slid out from under him, chairs have moved away as he sat down, and he has slipped off ladders and tripped over things that weren't there. Usually, the accidents occur when the strange footsteps are heard.

Probably the strangest thing that happened to Fred Weinstein was the time he was returning home to the Dakota and by chance looked up at his apartment from the street. Through his window he saw a huge crystal chandelier with dozens of lights glowing brilliantly. He took a second look for he had no such chandelier in his apartment. He scanned the side of the building again, recounting the floors. Yes, it was his apartment. There was no doubt about it. But he knew there was no crystal chandelier in his apartment. Thinking that perhaps his wife had installed it as a surprise, he rushed upstairs. He found no crystal chandelier. However, in the living-room ceiling where he had seen the chandelier, there were, under numerous coats of paint, the remains of a bracket that had once supported a chandelier.

Probably the most bizarre of all the Dakota's ghosts was the one first seen just before World War II and on a number of occasions since then. The Dakota was one of

New York's first residential buildings to have electricity during the gaslight era. The wiring and fixtures were, and in some places still are, quite antiquated. One of the Dakota's electricians was alone in the basement one night, trying to figure out something about the ancient circuitry. As he was thumbing through an old electrician's manual, a short man with a long nose, tiny wire-framed glasses, a gray beard minus a mustache, emerged from the darkness. He was wearing a frocklike coat with a wing collar and a high hat. He stepped up to the startled electrician, reached up under his gray top hat, pulled off the wig he was wearing, and shook it in the electrician's face. After this angry but silent demonstration, the little man vanished back into the shadows. The electrician was confronted by the wig-shaking stranger on four other occasions. Sometimes the stranger is seen only for a fleeting instant, standing motionless near the edge of the darkness.

Is the little man with a large nose and spectacles who steps out of the night a stranger? It could be that he has more right than anyone else to be at the Dakota. For Edward Clark, the man who started building and named it, only to die before it was completed, was a man of short stature, wore thin, steel-rimmed glasses, had a beard but no mustache, and wore a wig.

*One short sleep past, we wake eternally, and
death shall be no more: Death, thou shalt die!*
John Donne
("Death Be Not Proud")

18

The Ghosts of the Hosts

This is the gruesome story of a man who was put to
death in a heinous manner, and whose flesh was manufac-
tured into wallets in Morristown, New Jersey. Several of
the billfolds made in Morristown, U.S.A., exist today.
Yet, the "wallet man" knew even greater horror before
his death. Does his restless spirit still prowl the corridors
of a well-known eatery, the Wedgewood Inn? Many think
so. And do his icy fingers reach from beyond an unhallowed grave demanding retribution from the descendants
of the townspeople who perpetrated a ghastly punishment
against him for a crime he may or may not have committed? Let the reader be the judge.

In England, many of the older inns and pubs have their
"house ghosts" which are taken for granted and accepted
as part of the establishment. Likewise, a number of old
restaurants and taverns in the United States have their
"house ghosts," too.

The Wedgewood Inn is a beautiful, rambling structure
which had served as a Colonial inn and a farmhouse, but
now is a very chic restaurant. Its dining area was once the

farmhouse porch. Over the door that was previously the front entrance hung a sign that read "1749 A.D." There was also a large polished brass knocker in the form of a lion with a woman's head that appeared to be very old. A glorious sunburst design crowned the door.

Then, Luis Villacorta, the manager, glided noiselessly over toward us. He introduced the Wedgewood's attractive blonde hostess standing beside him as his wife.

Luis and his wife showed us the first floor and the notorious table number thirteen. Mrs. Villacorta explained, "On table number thirteen, a candle lights by itself when there's no one around. Each table has a candle, and we are careful to see that all of the candles are out before we close for the night. I've walked by table thirteen and put out the candle—only to discover it is still burning after checking the other rooms. We even changed the table number but it didn't help. Waitresses still report a lighted candle burning on this table when there shouldn't be one."

"Luis, has anything peculiar happened to you, here?" I asked.

"Only two really eerie things happened to me. I had closed up for the night and was walking to my car when I thought I saw a fire flickering in the window. I ran back inside and found a lit candle on table thirteen. Also, there are always problems with the electric lights. They turn on and off by themselves. But sometimes they just flicker— like a signal. It keeps happening even though we completely rewired the place some time ago.

"Most of the strange things happen upstairs in the Hamilton Room."

The second floor was dark except for the mysterious Hamilton Room. Fancy, Victorian-style, smoked-glass lights provided a dimly lit view of the room's rich interior. Brocade curtains in gold, blue and green covered the windows and accented the gold-patterned wallpapered room. Good reproductions added to the rooms attractiveness. A fireplace, painted green, centered the far wall. The sunburst design over the front door was repeated above the mantelpiece.

A waitress and the busboy entered with a tray of coffee and table service. The young man silently and efficiently set the huge rectangular table of the Hamilton Room as the waitress lit a sterling silver candelabrum that formed its centerpiece. The candles' flames faltered and flickered. Gradually, the room became cooler and cooler.

"The Hamilton Room used to be rented out to a private company on a daily basis. Every day for lunch, sixteen or seventeen employees would come here to eat. The same waitress always served them. She claimed funny things happened to her in this room when no one was around. Things like chills and other things she couldn't explain. It's always the coldest room in the whole restaurant. It gets uncomfortably cold at times, even on the nicest days.

"The employees have heard crazy sounds. One of my waitresses had a party downstairs, and she heard a whining, moaning sound coming from up here somewhere. All of my employees have heard it at one time or another, but that particular waitress said, 'It sounded like a soul in torment.'

"Maybe it's the soul of the girl who was murdered in this room. Her name was Phebe. She was a servant girl who lived in this house. She must have caught the hired hand robbing the place, so he killed her. He also murdered the couple who owned the house when they discovered him hiding in the barn. His name was Antoine Le Blanc, a French immigrant. The murder took place in 1833. He ran away after the killings. Several days later, the townspeople caught him as he was about to board a ship with the family's silverware. Le Blanc was tried for the murders and found guilty. But the sentence was pretty awful, even for this crime."

"What did they do to him?" I asked.

"Well, first they strung him up and let the guy strangle to death slowly. Then, he was skinned and wallets were made out of his tanned hide which were then sold as souvenirs. But that's not all. The town surgeon was ordered to cut the killer's dead body up in very small pieces before they finally got rid of it. The man didn't get a decent Christian burial, either. They just scattered the remains."

Our attention then focused on Peg, an employee at the restaurant. Peg volunteered this story:

"Another waitress was setting up the Hamilton Room one night after a big dinner party, getting it ready for the next day. The whole restaurant was empty. Then the girl heard the sound of heavy footsteps coming up the stairway to this room. She thought maybe I'd come back up to help her, but when she walked out of the room to see who it was, no one was there. She was completely alone. She told me she sensed that someone was here watching her, so she left right away. She didn't even finish with the room. I think she was really scared."

Bob Hunt, the assistant manager, said, "I can vouch for that! I get the same feeling that maybe I'm being watched. It's especially true when I'm working here by myself."

Josephine Lanza, another Wedgewood waitress said, "Yes, I know what you mean! We were setting up tables in the bar area one time and we saw a figure of a man breeze past. He looked real shadowy. It was in the corner of the bar where the crazy picture is.

"There's a print on the wall downstairs called Psyche at Nature's Window. There's a half-nude girl in it, with wings on her shoulders, looking down into a pool of water. Some of the employees have seen a woman's bloody hand reach out of that picture like it was trying to grab somebody."

Rosemary Torrick then offered her experiences: "I guess I'd have to say the strangest thing that happened was the time I was serving a party here in the Hamilton Room. I brought the coffee in at about ten o'clock. The Hamilton Room was the only one that was still in use on this floor that night. The boy was supposed to bring up a tray for me, and I saw the white form of a man out of the corner of my eye. Thinking it was the busboy, I turned around quickly but no one was there. I didn't hear footsteps or any other sounds—like a tray rattling or anything. Come to think about it, I should have known something strange was happening when I didn't hear footsteps! The form sort of floated out of sight. When I stepped out of the room to check the hall, it was completely empty and had turned icy cold, like I'd stepped into a deep freeze.

"And one afternoon down in the bar, I saw a man in

an overcoat and hat standing in the corner. I thought it was a customer. He just disappeared when I came toward him."

We interviewed a good cross section of the Inn's employees, and agreed that, indeed, the Wedgewood Inn shows every indication of being haunted. The workers told us of an old portrait that is repeatedly found inverted and no human agent claims responsibility. Standing near the entrance to the room, an employee said, "Hey, move your hand over this spot. This one little area—it's icy cold. Feel it!" Everyone there took turns passing their hands over the cold spot. We all felt the frigid energy mass. There was no air conditioner on in the room or any ducts near the spot. When we left to go downstairs, everyone felt as though we were being followed. The cold chill seemed to follow us and it didn't leave until we had reached the fireplace in the main dining room.

Should you have the opportunity to visit that elegant eating establishment, you won't find table number thirteen, for its number has been changed. However, if you are a persuasive talker, and have the nerve, Luis Villacorta might permit you to dine in the haunted Hamilton Room—at your own risk, of course.

There may be one in your neighborhood—a darkened abandoned building. When night approaches and shadows extend gloomy tentacles slowly across the breadth of a busy city street, be sure to avoid its murky sidewalks and alleys. For a cold sweat envelops the unwary passerby and a noticeable rapid heartbeat telegraphs a warning not to enter the cool shadows. For who knows what untold evil lurks there. Hurrying past such a building—by way of the opposite side of the street, there's often a feeling that someone—or something—is watching. Most of us take a quick furtive glance over a shoulder and rapidly walk away, ashamed of feeling such unjustified dread.

Why is it that many buildings seem to emanate an unholy presence at night? Perhaps it is as Gary B. Clark of Monterey, California, theorizes. Such buildings are nighttime abodes for visiting spirits—hotels for haunters! "Beings from other worlds know how beautiful our city is and they like to come and visit just like any other tourist. Maybe they're attracted to big empty buildings and occupy them even as the living seek refuge in hotels or motels as night approaches. It's reasonable to assume, should they choose to stay in habitats frequented by the living, that chaos would result," says Clark.

And, indeed, no one knows better than Gary the reality of such palpable terror. For it was by personal ordeal only four years ago that he learned the dreadful truth. While refurbishing an old building destined to become Casa Bodega, a liquor store and delicatessen, he witnessed face to face a visitation from the world of the dead. His chosen business site was haunted.

"I had goose pimples so high you could've cut them off with a razor blade," said Gary, as his eyes widened in solemn recall of one particular night's hair-raising events.

For weeks, minor incidents kept occurring. Paint brushes, saws and hammers mysteriously disappeared and reappeared only to be discovered in some area not readily accessible to humankind. Light switches concealed in unlikely places were extinguished at closing time. But in the morning when Clark returned, the lights were unexplainably turned on as if by a phantom hand. Mysterious footsteps were often heard from the second floor, sometimes making a loud walking sound and even jumping around as if dancing a jig. When glancing back at one's own shadow in the late afternoon, an extra disturbing silhouette would ominously appear.

All were alarming events. But both Clark and his wife stared in stark disbelief one day as they watched the full-sized figure of a man materialize before them, turn and walk right into a wall, then fade from sight. The ghost looked just like a living being. It had salt-and-pepper gray hair, stood better than six feet tall, weighed more than two hundred pounds and had a paunchy abdomen. The phantom was so clearly seen that Clark approximated the apparition's dimensions by comparing its size to his own proportions. Huge hands extended from the cuffs of a long-sleeved flannel shirt and gray work pants encased the totally visible but transparent body. "We were both so scared we could hardly breathe. My wife and I are rational, sane people. Both of us would swear to what we saw that day," said Clark.

He ran long slender fingers through a thicket of reddish-brown beard. His ruddy complexioned face and deep blue eyes became suddenly very animated as he continued. "I've been a volunteer fireman in Pacific Grove for years. Nothing frightens me as a rule. And I'm psychologically prepared for nearly anything. But enough is enough—important legal papers vanished. And the deli refrigerator case was repeatedly sabotaged. A small nut was constantly being loosened allowing the chemical coolant to escape.

"The night before the grand opening, I was stocking the cooler shelves with wine. There was a bottle in each hand when suddenly an unseen force whacked my arm behind the elbow and an expensive bottle of wine crashed to the floor. It was almost like a ceremonial christening.

"Objects moved by themselves. A bag of potato chips defied all natural laws of physics and flew off a rack landing halfway across the room."

He paused for a moment, as if gathering his thoughts, then began again. "It was very unnerving and kept getting worse. Incidents were occurring more frequently and intensifying in frightful quality. One of my customers who is also a neighbor was involved in an accident in front of the store one day. A whole load of fresh mackerel was dumped onto the street and sidewalk in front of my door. Well, I went out and did as much as possible to help. But the fishy smell was incredible and a slippery coat of slime was everywhere. A hose was needed to clean the mess. I walked back inside my store, locking the door to prevent onlookers from tracking ooze into my place of business. First, I phoned the police and then went to assist a customer at the cash register. After I took the man's money, this . . . thing, spirit, ghost or whatever, walked right by my elbow! There were no other customers in the store. It was a transparent person that moved real fast, right through a wall and into the street. It resembled the same gray-haired man my wife and I had seen before. But after I went outside, the thing came back into the building, or so I later discovered. My sister-in-law saw him. She was as white as a sheet. I asked her, 'What's the matter?' And she said, 'I saw it. A ghost! It came in, stood right by the window and watched you.' She described exactly the same apparition I'd seen earlier.

"And it happened again near the cash register. There was a peculiar sound. For a second I paused and listened. There I stood, counting quarters—suddenly, the hairs raised on the back of my neck. Someone or something was standing behind me and it was making a strange noise. Before I could turn and take a look, wham! Something hit my elbow and twelve or thirteen quarters flew everywhere!

"I'll admit I was scared. The old heart was beating hard. When I calmed down a little, I picked up the coins, counted the bills, made out a deposit and put the money in our safe. My nervous system couldn't stand the strain any longer. Because then, I got kind of brave and said, 'If there's a spirit here, give me a sign of your presence. If you're hostile, or an evil soul, get the hell out of here. I don't want anything to do with you. Quit bothering me. If you're friendly, I don't mind you being here but cut out the dirty tricks. All the little aggravations you're responsible for are bothering me and other people who work here. It's not fair because we can't bother you back. Now, if you want us to know you're here, there's got to be a better way. So, if you're here, show me.' "

No sooner were the words uttered than the uneasy brief silence was shattered by a hellish sound. It was as if some evil wind had entered the shuttered room from the depths of Hades. A roaring, more like a growling sound increased with each passing second. Gary stiffened in fear and dread. Frozen in anticipation of the horrid presence, he was unable to turn and look behind him—afraid of what might be there. His body hairs raised and his scalp began to tingle as if suddenly electrified. The intense sound permeated his being, controlled his motor responses. Suddenly, the terrifying spell was broken by a fierce chorus of flapping wings, hundreds of wings, becoming louder and louder. Huge birds from the dark distant prehistoric past might have sounded similar to the incredible crescendo that gathered around Gary Clark. Then the magnification of the flapping noise intensified to the extent that it became a loud whirring, like the noise made by a helicoper's rotor blades. "It was just awful," said Clark, shuddering in recollection, "like the wind roaring through a canyon—whoosssh! And that flapping sound . . . believe me, I was so horrified my heart actually hurt.

"When it was all over and I'd calmed down, I analyzed the situation. The ghost had given me ample proof of its presence. There's no way a sound like that could have just happened. Then I struck a bargain with the spirit. I said, 'If there's anything humanly possible that I can do for you, I'll do it. On the other hand, if you'd keep an eye on the store when I'm not present, I'd appreciate it.' Then, I left."

But incidents continued to occur and eventually, Gary Clark decided either he or the ghost would have to vacate the store. Clark called parapsychologist Mark Turck, a director of the International Ghost Registry. Turck brought his wife, Louise, a hypnotic trance medium, into the deli to investigate the haunting. Louise had not been informed of the particulars involved. During two separate trance inductions, Louise established contact with many haunters of Casa Bodega. Some were derelict souls, not realizing they were deceased. They had been initially attracted by Gary Clark's natural psychic sensitivity. Soul rescue, a process that assists such beings was attempted for those who were ready to be helped. Workers in spiritual realms contacted the wayward earthbound souls, using Louise's mediumship as a line of communication. Then, many were led to enter more fruitful activities in their own time and space.

One mischievous entity laid claim to creating most of the havoc at Casa Bodega revealing intimate details of events within the store only Clark knew. But the "electric man" seemed to play an extremely important part in the haunting. While out of body in a trance state, Louise's consciousness was upstairs where she met a character in spirit who had fiery sparks flying around him as if electrically charged. When she approached, the "electric man" screamed, "Help me, help me. Put out the fire!" Multicolored sparks crackled dangerously around the entity. Louise created a bucket of water (a thought form construct) and splashed him with its contents. The being crumbled to ashes and dust as she watched.

A bizarre accident once occurred at Casa Bodega that might reveal the true identity of the electrified specter. In 1967, while the edifice was being used by a noted inventive genius involved in scientific research, a violent explosion set off by an electrically charged solution with which he was working took the experimenter's life. The scientist's physical description closely matched that of the ghostly figure seen by Clark and two other witnesses. One can't be certain the accident victim haunts Casa Bodega but strong evidence points to the possibility.

Even though "house cleansing" or "purification" (exorcism) took place inside the building, entities still plagued Clark and many who worked there. Clark, after less than a year in the lucrative liquor and deli business abandoned the project and his ex-partner now runs the establishment. Many people interested in the bizarre have requested permission to stay all night in the haunted building. And it is possible to stay for as long . . . or as brief a period as you like. The owner does, however, require a refundable five-hundred-dollar cash deposit to cover breakage and other damage that might occur should the "electric man" or others of the many unsavory denizens who haunt there decide to visit a hapless investigator in the still blackness of a Monterey night.

I'm comin' back and haunt you, don't you fret.
What if I get as far as Hell away?
They's things of me that just can't help but stay—
Whether I want or not, you can't forget.

John V. A. Weaver
("Ghost")

19

The Haunted Elevator

Dorothy Jacobsen was a supervisory nurse and nursing instructor at Ellis Hospital in Schenectady. She was tops in her career but otherwise lived a secluded life. She paid little attention to her physical appearance, and wore outdated clothing and heavy, thick-heeled shoes. She was nearly forty years old but appeared closer to sixty. Dorothy's home was a dimly lit house with no radio or television and very little furniture.

Dorothy kept to herself most of the time and was always lonely, especially during the long, companionless nights. Then one night, alone and friendless, she felt she could no longer bear her social solitude. She died by her own hand.

Life for the staff at Ellis Hospital went on. Doctors, nurses, and technicians came and went. After a few months, Dorothy Jacobsen was forgotten except in a few individuals' private thoughts. Nurse Jacobsen may have been just about forgotten, but she wasn't gone.

Late one night, a nurse who had worked with Dorothy was waiting for an elevator. When elevator B-1 arrived and the doors opened, the nurse saw a familiar-looking nurse get off the elevator. When she realized how much the nurse looked like Dorothy, her late fellow worker, she followed her down the hall and saw her round a corner. When she herself rounded that same corner an instant later, the hall was empty.

Another nurse, who had been one of Dorothy's students, was riding in the same elevator. Something, which she couldn't explain, started her thinking about her old instructor. Then suddenly she looked at the polished metal of the wall of the elevator and saw Dorothy's image reflected there. The young nurse turned around. There was no one there. When she looked back at the polished metal wall, the reflection had disappeared. Suddenly the temperature in the elevator dropped at least ten degrees.

Robin Boston Barron, a filmmaker who does medical photography at Ellis Hospital, knew Nurse Jacobsen quite well. After her suicide, a young nursing student moved into Dorothy's house. Robin didn't see the girl for a year. When he finally saw the young nurse again, she was very depressed and talked about suicide. "She dressed just like Dottie—right down to the hairstyle," said Robin. "I told her to get out of that place, and she did."

Early one Friday, about six-forty-five in the morning, Robin was on his way to the operating room to photograph a new surgical technique. He arrived at the bank of elevators and pushed the button. When the doors of elevator B-1 opened, he entered and pushed the operating-room-floor button. The doors closed and the elevator began its ascent. Robin was sure that he had been alone when the doors closed. Yet, he felt that he was not alone. He turned around and saw a nurse standing in the corner. She looked familiar, but he didn't associate her with the late nursing instructor. That is, not until he took a second look. He didn't want to stare, but he was sure that his fellow passenger bore a remarkable resemblance to Dorothy Jacobsen.

"It was eerie," said Robin. "I waited for her to get off. But the elevator continued on up and didn't stop until it reached the sixth floor, where the operating room is. When I turned to let her exit ahead of me, I found that I was alone on the elevator. As I stood there in disbelief, the elevator got very cold. Then I began to detect a funny smell, like flowers—no, more like perfume."

Others have seen the specter of Dorothy in elevator B-1. Why does the ghost of Dorothy Jacobsen seem to want to spend eternity riding up and down in elevator B-1 at Ellis Hospital in Schenectady, New York?

Could it have anything to do with the fact that the nursing school was her whole life when she was alive, and that when she took her own life, she was no longer able to contribute to the saving of lives of others?

Is it possible that Nurse Jacobsen will continue her never-ending ride on elevator B-1, seeking in death the friends she never had in life?

Whatever the reason, you can be sure that the elevator at Ellis Hospital is not the only one that is haunted. The next time you're alone in an elevator, try thinking very hard about whether or not that conveyance is haunted. maybe something or someone will materialize.

Bibliography

Books

Life at the Dakota, Stephen Birmingham, Random House, 1979.

Ghosts Around the House, Susy Smith, World Publishing Co., 1970.

My Wicked Ways, Errol Flynn, Berkley Publishing Corp., 1959, Putnam.

The Two Lives of Errol Flynn, M. Freedland, Wm. Morrow Co., 1978.

From the Devil's Triangle to the Devil's Jaw, R. A. Winer, Bantam, 1977.

Historic Preservation in Illinois. Illinois History (no pub. data.)

Cavern of Crime, Judy Magee, *The Livingston Ledger*, Smithland, Ky., 1973.

Dark and Bloodied Ground, Mary Bolte, Hawthorn, 1973.

Weird America, Jim Brandon, Dutton, 1978.

The Hidden Spectre, R. Tralins, Avon Books, 1970.

Supernatural On Stage, R. Huggett, Taplinger, 1975.

Psychic Pets, J. Wylder, Stonehill Publ. Co., N.Y., 1978.

Strangest of All, F. Edwards, Ace Books, 1959.

Invisible Horizons, V. Gaddis, Chelton, 1965.

The Strongest Poison, Mark Lane, 1980, Hawthorn.

Six Years with God, J. Mills, 1979, A & W Pub., Inc.

By Lust Possessed, Eric Lombard, editor, Signet, 1980.

The Entity, F. DeFelitta, Warner Books, 1979.

Witches and Witchcraft, J. Kingston, Danbury Press, 1976.

Witchcraft, Magic and the Supernatural, Various Authors, Octopus Books, London, 1974.

Jayne Mansfield and the American 50's, Martha Saxton, Houghton Mifflin, 1975.

The Witchcraft Report, Hans Holzer, Ace, 1973.

Man, Myth and Magic, A compilation (encyclopedia), Marshall Cavendish Corp., 1970.

Jayne Mansfield, A Biography, Mary Man, Drake, Inc., 1973.

Satanic Bible, Anton La Vey, Avon, 1969.

The Supernatural, The Danbury Press (encyclopedia), Grolier Enterprises, Inc., 1975.

Psychic World of California, D. St. Clair, Doubleday, 1972.

Magazines and Periodicals

Iliniwek, Vol. 10, No. 3, May–June 1972 (Old Slave House).

Morning Star, Rockford, Ill., 11–1–78 (Old Slave House).

Commercial Appeal, Memphis, Tenn., 11–1–78 (Old Slave House).

Modern People, 11–14–74 (Old Slave House), Franklin Park, Ill.

Family Digest, May, 1974 (Old Slave House; a Catholic monthly).

Grit, Family Section, 7–29–73, p. 13, Grover Brinkman (Old Slave House).

Kentucky News, Commonwealth of Kentucky, Dept. of Public Info., Frankfort, Ky. "Liberty Hall's Spectacular Specters," by Paula Alexander, States News Bureau. (A report on the ghosts of Liberty Hall).

Automobile Bulletin, "Let the Spirit Move You . . . To Where the Ghosts Are," September–October, 1970.

Memoirs of John M. Mason, Jacob Van Cechten, p. 476, 477. New York, March 4, 1818 (an account of Mrs. Varick's death).

Memphis Magazine, 1979, David Dawson, "The Ghost in Seat C-5."

Fort Lauderdale News and Sun-Sentinel, Sunday, Dec. 31, 1978, an article by Patricia Koza, "National Theater has Unusual 'Extra.' "

Waiting in the Wings

The Nashville Tennessean, Sunday, June 4, 1978, "Ann H. Adjusts to 'The Lady,' " Eugene Wyatt.

The Tennessean Magazine, May 1978, Bill Reed and Gene Wyatt, "Who Is 'The Lady' Who Torments Ann H?"

National Enquirer, "My Life of Terror—Tormented by a Fiendish Spirit," 1979, Harold Lewis.

Midnight/Globe, various publications. (Re: Jim Jones story).

National Enquirer, various publications. (Re: Jim Jones story).

Death, August 1978, "Jayne Mansfield's Ghost."

Index

ABOUT THE AUTHORS

More Haunted Houses is RICHARD WINER's fifth book. His previous works are about mysteries of the sea, such as the bestseller *The Devil's Triangle*.

He is a graduate of the University of Minnesota and spent most of his working life in the news media and photography. He has also been a professional sailor, treasure hunter, yachtsman, hobo and soldier of fortune. His collection of vintage automobiles include a Pierce Arrow, several classic Packards, a Bugatti and some early sports racing cars.

NANCY OSBORN ISHMAEL was born August 26, 1939, in East Chicago, Indiana. Mrs. Ishmael resides in Florida with her three children, Jack, Russ and Julie. She attended Indiana University and Broward Community College, North campus, majoring in psychology. She has also attended the Arthur Ford Academy in Coral Gables, Florida and completed a course in parapsychology and mediumship. For more than eight years, Nancy Osborn Ishmael has studied the paranormal in the laboratory and in the field. She gives lectures and does radio and TV appearances of topics of the supernatural. She welcomes letters and comments. Please be sure to enclose a stamped, self-addressed envelope if a reply is desired.

A Special Preview of
the chilling first pages of

HAUNTED HOUSES

By
Richard Winer
and
Nancy Osborn Ishmael

Eerie tours of the unexplainable
by the authors of
MORE HAUNTED HOUSES

Pocahontas' body, lovely as a poplar,
Sweet as a red haw in November
Or a paw paw in May,
Did she wonder? Does she remember? . . .
In the dust, in the cool tombs?

Carl Sandburg

1

The Haw Branch Hauntings

Some thirty miles west of Richmond, Virginia, along U.S. Highway 360, lies a small town, not much more than a hamlet, called Amelia, Virginia. Ask anyone in Amelia, a mechanic at one of the two garages, the clerk at the only hotel or some passerby on the main street, how to get to Haw Branch. They are friendly folks and will gladly tell you. They know well of the old plantation. They know that strange things have been going on at Haw Branch for a long time.

The Haw Branch plantation dates back to pre-Revolutionary War days. There are no records of the area before 1735. But what chronicles now exist show that the manor house was built prior to that year. It could date back to the 1720's, and that part of it which was once an old inn may date back even earlier. To visit Haw Branch today is to enter a time machine and journey back to long, long ago.

The Haw Branch manor house is one of the most traditional homes in Virginia. It is situated on a long hill and set in a brick-paved depression resembling an ancient moat. The gleaming white three-and-a-half-story structure, with its towering chimneys, is surrounded by acres of rolling lawn and ancient magnolia, elm and tulip trees. Occasional gardens break the lawn's carpet effect. Outbuildings include the early kitchen (during the ante-bellum era, cooking was done in a building separate from the main house), a barn, a smokehouse and the old slave quarters—all restored. There is even a former private school on the grounds.

At one time, the whole plantation covered over fifteen thousand acres; and as many as five hundred slaves are believed to have worked there. The slaves were apparently well treated, for after the emancipation a number chose to stay on. There are two graveyards—one for family members and one for colored. Today, Haw Branch covers around two thousand acres.

If the grounds have the appearance of another era, then walking up the steps to the porch and entering the manor house may convince you that you are actually back in pre-Civil War days. Except for plumbing and electrical fixtures, the house is pure ante-bellum . . . with canopied beds, authentic wing-back chairs, handmade rugs, vintage utensils, a grandfather's clock and early family portraits. One of these portraits, the one hanging over the fireplace in the library, has a very bizarre history.

As you stand in the library at Haw Branch, something seems to draw your eyes toward the portrait of a beautiful young woman that hangs over the fireplace. The woman in the painting is Florence Wright, who lived in Duxbury, Massachusetts many years ago. The twenty-year-old woman's bright blue eyes sparkle below a crown of reddish brown hair. Her complexion has the appearance of living flesh. The green chair she sits in is upholstered in a shade of green even darker than the jade-colored vase on the table next to her. The soft pink rose in the vase looks real. The picture is contained in a huge hand-carved wooden frame.

Admiring the portrait of the beautiful young woman, a viewer would find it hard to believe that the painting is shrouded in mystery. Certainly I had no premonition that such is the case, as I looked up at the picture. Then the owners of Haw Branch told me the story:

Cary McConnaughey and his wife Gibson purchased Haw Branch in 1964. Mrs. McConnaughey hadn't seen the plantation since she was a child when her grandmother, Harriet Mason Jefferson, lived there. Her family had owned Haw Branch since before the American Revolution. It had been almost half a century since any of Gibson McConnaughey's family lived in the manor house.

When the McConnaugheys visited the plantation in 1964, the mansion was virtually in shambles from fifty years of neglect. After deciding that the building was restorable, they bought it and began an extensive restoration project. Then, on August 13, 1965, the McConnaugheys, their children and two dogs moved into the plantation house.

It was four years later that Gibson was given the portrait of Florence Wright by an elderly cousin. The girl in the painting was a distant relative connected by marriage. All the cousin knew was that when Florence's parents were alive, they had a summer home in Massachusetts, and that just before the painting was finished the young woman had suddenly died. The artist, whose name was forgotten, completed the work after the subject's death. During her short life Florence Wright never visited Haw Branch.

When the cousin gave the portrait to the McConnaughey's, she told them it was a beautifully colored pastel painting. After uncrating it and painstakingly cleaning the glass, they discovered what appeared to be a charcoal rendering of dirty white, gray and black rather than a colored painting. They could find no signature of the artist. The back was tightly sealed and they left it that way.

A few days after the portrait in its heavy frame was hung over the library fireplace, Gibson (Mrs. McConnaughey) was in the basement when she heard, coming from the library, the voices of several women engaged in conversation. Thinking it was probably some friends who had come to visit, she went upstairs, calling out, "I'm coming right up." She heard the voices until just before she reached the library. When she entered the room, there was no one there. Furthermore, she could find no one anywhere throughout the big house. And there were no cars in the parking area.

In February 1970, a few months later, Cary McConnaughey was seated in the library reading the Sunday paper. Glancing up, he noticed that the rose in the portrait was turning pink right before his eyes. He got up and walked over to the picture. He could see also that the girl's black hair was gradually beginning to lighten, and that her grayish skin was turning flesh-colored. In fact, nearly all of the blacks and grays in the portrait were taking on color. The changes continued slowly day by day. In the meantime, voices of young women talking and laughing were again heard coming from the library from time to time. But the origin of the sounds could never be found. With the passing of each day, the pastel hues became more obvious. It was only a matter of months before the colorless portrait was transformed into its present pastel brilliance.

A clairvoyant who lived in a neighboring county heard of the portrait that had changed color and called on the McConnaugheys. After studying the picture, he said that

Florence Wright's spirit was permanently bound to the portrait because she died before it was completed, and that she had the power to remove the color from it when she was dissatisfied with where it hung. The spirit apparently accompanied the girl's portrait to Haw Branch.

Florence Wright liked Haw Branch. So, with help from the spirits of two other young women, she restored the original color to her portrait. After the color had finally returned to the picture, the voices of the young women were not heard any more.

But there was more that would happen with the portrait of Florence Wright. In Gibson McConnaughey's own words, this is what occurred.

"One of our daughters and a visiting friend were sitting on the floor beneath the portrait as the family watched television about seven o'clock one summer night in 1972. The two girls decided to move over to the sofa, and less than one minute after they moved, the supports of the picture's heavy frame pulled loose. Then, as though a slow-motion camera was recording the scene, the portrait slowly slid down the wall until the bottom of the frame reached the mantel shelf where it crushed a row of porcelain antiques. The picture tipped forward slightly, slipped over the edge of the mantel and fell to the wide pine floorboards.

"As everyone in the room sat transfixed, staring in disbelief, there was a jarring bump and the tinkle of breaking glass that sent Smokey, our cat, yowling across the room in fright. The portrait had fallen face down on the exact spot where the girls had been sitting, making a dent in the floor. Broken glass was everywhere.

"Although the painting itself was undamaged, the big wooden frame was broken. Lifting it up, we found underneath what had been the tightly sealed backing of the frame, a brass plate that gave the girl's full name, her birth date in Duxbury, Massachusetts, and her date of death in the same place. Though we searched carefully for the artist's signature both on the front and the back of the painting, it could not be found."

As Gibson shifted her weight in the wing-back chair she was sitting in, she continued her story. "Next day, the frame was repaired, the portrait placed back in it and the glass replaced. The man who did the work searched as carefully as we had searched to find the artist's signature, but with no success.

"It was late in the day when we arrived back at Haw Branch with the portrait. The sun was low in the sky. As my husband and I lifted the picture from the back of the station wagon, I happened to tilt my end of the frame slightly upward. Suddenly, as though a red neon sign had been lit, the name, 'J. Wells Champney,' appeared. It had been signed in pencil on the apron of the dark mahogany table in the picture. Only under a certain angle of light could it be seen."

Cary McConnaughey now took over the story. "We learned that the beautiful woman in the portrait had been born into a wealthy family that owned several homes, including the one at Duxbury. Her parents commissioned Mr. Champney to paint the portrait. Then one day, when the painting was well along the way to completion, Florence Wright, twenty-four years old, was practicing at her piano. Suddenly she slumped over the keyboard. She died almost immediately from a massive stroke.

"The artist completed the portrait and added the partially opened rose to signify that his subject died an untimely death before the painting was completed.

"And do you know," added Gibson, "many people who come to Haw Branch and see Florence Wright's portrait say they can see a pink flush steal up her throat and spread to her cheeks!"

"Did you learn more about the artist?" I asked.

"He was killed when he fell down an elevator shaft in New York City," said Cary.

Although the mysterious incidents surrounding the portrait of Florence Wright are beyond the bounds of ordinary knowledge, they were not terrifying per se. But horror and fright have prevailed at Haw Branch.

Early in the pre-dawn darkness of November 23, 1965, the entire McConnaughey family was awakened by a woman's blood-curdling scream that seemed to come from upstairs. Rushing up the steps from their first-floor bedroom, Gibson and Cary found their children gathered at the foot of the staircase that leads from the second floor to the attic. The children had decided that the scream originated in the attic. Porkchop and Blackie, the family's two dogs, were shaking with terror. No one volunteered to check the attic until well into the daylight hours, when nothing amiss was found there. This incident occurred three months after the McConnaugheys moved into Haw Branch, and it was the first inkling they had that something might be seriously wrong in the manor.

In February, a few months later, all six members of the McConnaughey family were sitting in the library watching television one night when they heard a jolting thud from outdoors that shook the house. "It sounded as though a very heavy solid object such as a safe had fallen from a great height and landed on the bricks of the moat that surrounds the house," said Gibson McConnaughey. "We rushed outside with flashlights, expecting to find something lying there. But nothing unusual was found."

The sound of a heavy object falling into the moat has been heard both at regular and irregular intervals ever since. On some occasions, it occurs during daylight hours.

Investigation by the McConnaugheys has revealed that previous residents also experienced the same weird happenings. (To our knowledge the last thumping occurred several weeks before Nancy and I visited Haw Branch in July 1978.)

On May 23, 1966, six months to the day since the McConnaugheys heard the scream in the night, a woman's anguished scream again echoed through the halls of Haw Branch. And, as in the previous incident, no source for the sound could be located.

Six months later, on November 23, the terrifying shriek of a woman's voice again resounded through Haw Branch just before dawn. This time Porkchop jumped into an open chest and Blackie buried himself under a blanket on the bed.

Then, shortly before dawn of May 23, 1967, exactly six months to the day since the last shrieking occurrence, the woman's scream from the attic was heard once more.

During the summer of 1967, Gibson and her husband were sitting up late one night reading. Shortly after one, Cary went to bed. Gibson stopped off in the kitchen to get a glass of milk. Except for an upstairs light the house was dark. As Gibson opened the refrigerator door and the inside light dimly lit the hall between the kitchen and the library, she happened to glance into the hall where something caught her eye: "I could plainly see the silhouette of a slim girl in a floor-length dress with a full skirt. It was not the wide fullness of a hoopskirt, but one from an earlier period. I could see no features but she was not transparent, just a white silhouette. I saw her for perhaps ten seconds. In the next instant she was gone. There was no gradual fading away; she simply disappeared from one instant to the next.

"I rushed to our bedroom and told my husband what I had seen. He laughed so hard that I didn't mention it to anyone else."

Several days later, one of the McConnaughey daughters approached her mother with the report of another harrowing visitation. When the daughter told her story, she knew absolutely nothing of what her mother had seen several nights previously.

The daughter began talking: "Blackie's barking on the front porch kept me awake last night, so I went downstairs and let her in. She scampered right past me and into the drawing room. When I looked into the drawing room, Blackie was sitting there wagging her tail and looking up at a lady in white who was standing in front of the fireplace. Before I could say anything the lady disappeared right in front of my eyes."

Gibson McConnaughey later found out that previous residents of Haw Branch had also seen "The Lady in White." At a family reunion the subject was brought up, and an older relative mentioned the fact that their great grandmother, Harriet B. Mason, had told of having seen the White Lady. She had even been awakened out of a sound sleep by a touch from the apparition.

There are times at Haw Branch when, instead of seeing the apparition of "The Lady in White," footsteps are heard descending from the attic to the second floor. Immediate investigations have disclosed only empty stairways.

On other occasions, lights have gone on by themselves when the names of certain ancestors who lived on the plantation in centuries past were mentioned. Sometimes lights that are already on go off for the same reason.

And there have been instances when the aroma of oranges being peeled, or roses, have permeated parts of the house, when actually no roses or oranges were on the premises.

The odor of fresh oranges was first noticed in November 1967. At the time only canned, frozen orange juice was in the house and all of the cans were unopened. Later that same week the McConnaughey family was sitting around the dinner table discussing the aromas. Gibson mentioned the name of her great grandmother, Harriet Mason, and immediately two bulbs in the electric chandelier over the dining room table grew extremely brilliant, almost like photo flashlights, and then they went out.

A week later, on November 23, realizing that it was again that time of the year for the mysterious woman's pre-dawn scream to be heard, the family made preparations for the coming event with several flashlights and a tape recorder. From midnight to dawn, they took turns staying awake. The two dogs and the cat behaved very nervously, but the scream was not heard that night.

On May 23, 1968, the McConnaugheys again waited, this time with flashlights and a tape recorder. While waiting for the scream, the entire family heard something walking across the yard with heavy footsteps. At the same time an eerie screeching wail penetrated the night.

"When the heavy footsteps began," Gibson said, "my husband and I attempted to step quietly out onto the porch to see what it was. We heard something running heavily, and in a matter of only several seconds, heard the call come from beyond the barn.

"Next morning our son and one daughter reported that they saw a giant bird standing in the yard in the moonlight under their windows. It was standing there with its wings spread out, appearing to have a wingspan of over six feet."

Although the woman's screams were never heard again, the screech of the giant bird was heard on a number of occasions, but the bird itself hasn't been seen since. The screeches were always heard only on the twenty-third of May or November. However, at the time of this writing, it's been several years since the family has heard the screech of the giant night bird.

Ever since the McConnaugheys moved into Haw

Branch, a number of untraceable noises have been heard in the manor house and on the surrounding grounds.

One May night in 1972, McConnaughey's son and some young friends were sleeping in the old slave quarters building. Throughout the night they kept hearing cowbells coming from the pasture. Yet, each time they looked out, there would be nothing there. Sometimes the sound of the cowbell would actually seem to encircle the building, but still their flashlights showed only an empty pasture. At that time there were no cows at Haw Branch Plantation.

There was also an occasion when what looked like a man carrying a lighted kerosene lantern emerged from the barn. The light was bobbing as it neared the house. As it passed the porch, there was no man to be seen—only the moving lantern. It rounded the corner of the house and vanished.

Not only are the sounds of a heavy object falling into the moat still heard at Haw Branch, but so are other noises—especially from the attic. Ever since the family moved into the old mansion, the children, who sleep upstairs, have told of hearing noises like furniture being moved around in the attic above their rooms. Even when the elder McConnaugheys slept upstairs, they, too, could hear the noise that sounded like furniture being dragged across the attic floor. Subsequent investigations revealed that all of the dust-covered furniture stored in the attic was unmoved. There were no traces of small animals or birds that might possibly have gotten inside the house.

An old rocking chair stored in the same attic is sometimes heard to rock in the night. Yet the chair is broken and would support no one.

At other times, a strange humming sound is heard in the basement. Once Mrs. McConnaughey wrote down the tune: C - C - B Flat - B Flat - C - C - E Flat, C - C - B

Flat - B Flat - A Flat. A musician friend who listened to the melody said it closely resembled an old English folk tune.

Is the answer to the Haw Branch mystery contained in the attic of the house? Possibly, but it's also conceivable that the answer lies in the basement. For down below is a sealed room—a chamber measuring approximately four by six feet and completely closed off by brick and masonry. It is a room that seems to hold some strange fascination for the McConnaughey dogs and cat.

A woman's terrifying scream just before dawn; a kerosene lantern floating across the yard; cowbells from phantom cows; the sound of moving furniture from furniture that isn't moved; the sound of a very heavy object falling, after which no object can be found; footsteps in the night; the ghostly woman in white; a tragically bizarre portrait; dogs terrified by something unseen; a giant man-sized bird with a blood-curdling screech—what horrible trauma could have occurred at Haw Branch in years past to bring these unexplainable things about? What deep, dark secret does the house hold—a house whose previous owner died suddenly just a few hours after signing over the deed . . . ?

This is but one of the amazing stories of ghosts, visitors from the dead, demonic curses and terrors from the beyond that are found in this Bantam Book, available wherever paperbacks are sold.

OUT OF THIS WORLD!

That's the only way to describe Bantam's great series of science fiction classics. These space-age thrillers are filled with terror, fancy and adventure and written by America's most renowned writers of science fiction. Welcome to outer space and have a good trip!

☐	14774	THE MARTIAN CHRONICLES by Ray Bradbury	$2.50
☐	13695	SOMETHING WICKED THIS WAY COMES by Ray Bradbury	$2.25
☐	14274	THE MAN WHO FELL TO EARTH by Walter Tevis	$2.25
☐	14323	STAR TREK: THE NEW VOYAGES by Culbreath & Marshak	$2.25
☐	13260	ALAS BABYLON by Pat Frank	$2.25
☐	14124	A CANTICLE FOR LEIBOWITZ by Walter Miller, Jr.	$2.50
☐	13312	SUNDIVER by David Brin	$1.95
☐	13999	THE INTEGRATED MAN by Michael Berlyn	$1.95
☐	13766	THE FARTHEST SHORE by Ursula LeGuin	$2.25
☐	14946	THE TOMBS OF ATUAN by Ursula LeGuin	$2.50
☐	14863	A WIZARD OF EARTHSEA by Ursula LeGuin	$2.50
☐	13563	20,000 LEAGUES UNDER THE SEA by Jules Verne	$1.75
☐	20147	FANTASTIC VOYAGE by Isaac Asimov	$2.25
☐	14268	RE-ENTRY by Paul Preuss	$2.25
☐	14156	VALIS by Philip K. Dick	$2.25

Buy them at your local bookstore or use this handy coupon for ordering:

Bantam Books, Inc., Dept. SF, 414 East Golf Road, Des Plaines, Ill. 60016

Please send me the books I have checked above. I am enclosing $_____ (please add $1.00 to cover postage and handling). Send check or money order —no cash or C.O.D.'s please.

Mr/Mrs/Miss_____

Address_____

City_____State/Zip_____

SF—7/81

Please allow four to six weeks for delivery. This offer expires 1/82.

FANTASY AND SCIENCE FICTION FAVORITES

Bantam brings you the recognized classics as well as the current favorites in fantasy and science fiction. Here you will find the beloved Conan books along with recent titles by the most respected authors in the genre.

☐	01166	URSHURAK	
		Bros. Hildebrandt & Nichols	$8.95
☐	14844	NOVA Samuel R. Delany	$2.50
☐	13534	TRITON Samuel R. Delany	$2.50
☐	14861	DHALGREN Samuel R. Delany	$3.95
☐	13127	TALES FROM GAVAGAN'S BAR	$1.95
		de Camp & Pratt	
☐	13837	CONAN & THE SPIDER GOD #5	$2.25
		de Camp & Pratt	
☐	13831	CONAN THE REBEL #6 Paul Anderson	$2.25
☐	14532	HIGH COUCH OF SILISTRA	$2.50
		Janet Morris	
☐	13670	FUNDAMENTAL DISCH Disch	$2.50
☐	13189	DRAGONDRUMS Anne McCaffrey	$2.25
☐	14127	DRAGONSINGER Anne McCaffrey	$2.50
☐	14204	DRAGONSONG Anne McCaffrey	$2.50
☐	14031	MAN PLUS Frederik Pohl	$2.25
☐	11736	FATA MORGANA William Kotzwinkle	$2.95
☐	11042	BEFORE THE UNIVERSE	$1.95
		Pohl & Kornbluth	
☐	13860	TIME STORM Gordon R. Dickson	$2.50
☐	13400	SPACE ON MY HANDS Frederic Brown	$1.95
☐	13996	THE PLANET OF TEARS Trish Reinius	$1.95

Buy them at your local bookstore or use this handy coupon for ordering:

We Deliver!
And So Do These Bestsellers.

☐	13826	**THE RIGHT STUFF** by Tom Wolfe	$3.50
☐	20229	**LINDA GOODMAN'S SUN SIGNS**	$3.95
☐	14431	**THE THIRD WAVE** by Alvin Toffler	$3.95
☐	14130	**GARY COOPER, AN INTIMATE BIOGRAPHY** by Hector Arce	$2.75
☐	01350	**SOME MEN ARE MORE PERFECT THAN OTHERS** by Merle Shain	$4.95
☐	01203	**WHEN LOVERS ARE FRIENDS** by Merle Shain	$3.95
☐	14965	**I'M DANCING AS FAST AS I CAN** by Barbara Gordon	$2.95
☐	14675	**THE BOOK OF LISTS** by D. Wallechinsky, I. & A. Wallace	$3.50
☐	13101	**THE BOOK OF LISTS #2** by I. Wallace, D. Wallechinsky, A. & S. Wallace	$3.50
☐	13111	**THE COMPLETE SCARSDALE MEDICAL DIET** by Herman Tarnover & S. Baker	$2.75
☐	14481	**THE ONLY INVESTMENT GUIDE YOU'LL EVER NEED** by Andrew Tobias	$2.75
☐	20138	**PASSAGES** by Gail Sheehy	$3.95
☐	14379	**THE GREATEST MIRACLE IN THE WORLD** by Og Mandino	$2.25
☐	14732	**ALL CREATURES GREAT AND SMALL** by James Herriot	$3.50
☐	13406	**THE MEDUSA AND THE SNAIL** Lewis Thomas	$2.95
☐	12942	**JOAN CRAWFORD: A BIOGRAPHY** by Bob Thomas	$2.75
☐	14422	**THE PILL BOOK** by Dr. Gilbert Simon & Dr. Harold Silverman	$3.50
☐	01137	**THE PEOPLE'S ALMANAC #2** by D. Wallechinsky & I. Wallace	$9.95
☐	14500	**GUINNESS BOOK OF WORLD RECORDS—19th Ed.** by McWhirter	$3.50

Buy them at your local bookstore or use this handy coupon for ordering:

Bantam Books, Inc., Dept. NFB, 414 East Golf Road, Des Plaines, Ill. 60016

Please send me the books I have checked above. I am enclosing $_____
(please add $1.00 to cover postage and handling). Send check or money order
—no cash or C.O.D.'s please.

Mr/Mrs/Miss_____

Address_____

City_____State/Zip_____

NFB—7/81

Please allow four to six weeks for delivery. This offer expires 1/82.

RELAX!
SIT DOWN
and Catch Up On Your Reading!

Bantam Book Catalog

Here's your up-to-the-minute listing of over 1,400 titles by your favorite authors.

This illustrated, large format catalog gives a description of each title. For your convenience, it is divided into categories in fiction and non-fiction—gothics, science fiction, westerns, mysteries, cookbooks, mysticism and occult, biographies, history, family living, health, psychology, art.

So don't delay—take advantage of this special opportunity to increase your reading pleasure.

Just send us your name and address and 50¢ (to help defray postage and handling costs).